Becoming
The Best Me

Dr. Robert Orndorff

First Edition

jaz
publishing

Becoming
The Best Me

Written by Robert Orndorff
Edited by Mary Lou Orndorff
Book and cover design by Sean Barr

Book Purchasing and Correspondence to:
Robert Orndorff
JAZ Publishing
State College PA
(814) 360-1633
Bob@JAZpublishing.com

ISBN 0-9729457-0-9
PRINTED IN THE UNITED STATES OF AMERICA

Table of Contents

About the Author – Dr. Robert Orndorff

Dr. Robert Orndorff is the Associate Director of Career Services and Affiliate Assistant Professor of Counselor Education at Penn State University. Bob received a doctoral degree in counselor education (specializing in career development) from Penn State University. Dr. Orndorff has authored articles on career planning and placement and has been published in a national journal, the *Journal of Counseling and Development*, published in national online publications (*CareerPlanit* and *College Parents of America*) and quoted in both the *U.S. News & World Report* and *Newsweek.*

Recently, Bob was the sole author of *The Unofficial Guide to Finding the Perfect Job,* published in February 2000 by IDG Books Worldwide, Inc., and re-published by Peterson's in October 2000 as *The Insider's Guide to Finding the Perfect Job.* In addition, Bob was asked to write a featured job search article in *Job Choices 2003*, a magazine published by the National Association of Colleges and Employers that is distributed annually (over 600,000) to most colleges and universities in America.

Bob has worked at four other college career centers: Indiana University of Pennsylvania, Georgetown University, Moravian College, and Elon University. While at Georgetown, Bob's program, *The Strategic Job Search*, won a national award for "the best educational program related to career services in the nation" and was highlighted on *Good Morning America.*

In addition to working in higher education, Bob is a career consultant in business and in education, particularly related to career education initiatives. Bob consults with Hershey High School in Pennsylvania, presenting a seminar called *College-4-Career* to high school students and their parents. He also served as the lead consultant with the Alamance-Burlington (North Carolina) Area Schools on developing and implementing a comprehensive career development program (K-12).

Acknowledgments

With all of the disheartening events recently taking place in our world beginning on September 11, 2001, I was committed to doing my part in providing at least a glimmer of hope and inspiration to our most precious American resource – our youth. This book, *Becoming The Best Me*, is therefore dedicated to my daughters Jessie (5) and Addie (3), and to my newborn son Zach. Thank you kids for making my #1 goal in life crystal clear: Becoming the Best DAD! But the book is also dedicated **to their cousins**: Rocky, Julie, Bo, Olivia, Brooke, Andrew, Bennett, Brooke, David, Nathan, Derek, Dana, Isaac, Tanner, Brayden, Devin, Hannah, Connor, Shane, Kaitlin, Emily, Kim; **to their little friends**: Cassidy, Ryan, Carlee, Jake, Kyle, Alison, Nathan, Caleb, Tyler, Madeline, Emma, Madelyn, Ryan, Meredith, Austin, Henry, Annabelle, Michael, Sara, Nicholas, Reaney, Thomas, Samuel, Tyler, Jessica, Calli, Sara, Jacob, Emily, Hannah, Madeline, Elli, Jake, Alia, Neil, Anna, Rachel, Michael, Jonathan, Jordan, Madison, Riley, Kara, Tyler, Lauren; and **to every child** – not only in America, but as my kids say it, "in the whole wide world!"

Thank you to my cousins Art and Dave, brother-in-law Pete, and friend Keith for serving our country and fighting for a better world for our kids. A special thank you to my talented, young graphic design specialist, Sean Barr, a recent Penn State grad, for creating a dynamic cover and for graphically laying out the entire book! I also want to thank my eight company contacts who helped me round up the employer views offered in this book: Betsy Lau, Accenture; Al Pollard, Enterprise Rent-A-Car; Phil Bues, IBM; Al Capps, Jefferson Pilot; Collene Burns, Microsoft; DeDe Dunevant, Peace Corps; Matt Hamlet, PricewaterhouseCoopers; and Kristin Dempsey, Verizon.

The people I owe the most gratitude are my family members, for writing and self-publishing this book was truly a family effort. Thanks first to my wife, Chris (Special Education certified), who always is willing to hear an earful, to proof my chapters, and to offer her professional opinion. Thanks to my three kids for inspiring me to start my own publishing company – JAZ Publishing – standing for Jessie, Addie, and Zach respectively. Thanks to my sister Kelly, a high school math teacher, for contributing content to the book. Thanks to my brother Erik, a middle-school teacher, for also contributing to the book's content and for helping to market the book. Thanks to my Dad, Bob, for coming up with the book's title and for helping with the editing. And a very special thanks to my Mom, Mary Lou, a recently retired middle school English Teacher, who found a second career as an exceptional editor-in-chief!

Finally, this book was written in the memory and spirit of Grandma Orndorff who recently passed away. This book's for you Grammy O!

A Note to Teachers, Counselors, & Administrators

Education is a central part of my life. In addition to serving as a career counselor, instructor, and administrator over the past 13 years, I am surrounded by family in education (wife – special education; mother – retired middle school English teacher; father – retired college administrator; sister – high school Math teacher; brother – elementary & middle school teacher; Aunt – guidance counselor; Uncle – assistant principal). While writing this book, I have received varying degrees of input from each of these family members. Needless to say, *Becoming The Best Me* was written from the heart!

Following are my thoughts and feelings regarding *why* this book is worthwhile and *who* can benefit from this book.

Why This Book?

Focus on those Educational & Extracurricular
OUTCOMES which are Highly Valued by Companies
The 7 "Essentials" (Outcomes) featured in this book are the skills, qualities, attitudes, and experiences that students must develop and subsequently utilize throughout their entire educational career in order to be marketable to prospective employers. As such, they are CAREER ESSENTIALS as well as LIFE ESSENTIALS -- OUTCOMES of a successful educational and extracurricular program. Although there are hundreds of worthwhile books out there helping students become aware of career options, they focus only on the process of *choosing* one's career – not on the process of *succeeding* in one's career. The 7 Career and Life Essentials which are examined and discussed not only make graduating students marketable for jobs but also empower them to be successful not only in their careers but also in their lives. In other words, these 7 Essentials which are sought after by recruiters in interviews are the same seven essentials found in the most successful people, both in work and in life.

Developmental, Seamless Approach from K – 12
The 7 Career and Life Essentials consist of skills, qualities, experiences, and attitudes that students can begin developing as early as kindergarten and continue refining all the way through to their senior year and beyond. The 7 Essentials can naturally be incorporated into any K-12 Career Development Plan. For example, *Communication* (one of the 7 Essentials) is a skill that can be practiced by 1st graders, 6th graders, and 12th graders alike, in developmentally appropriate ways.

Direct Advice from Top Company Recruiters Nationwide
Recruiters from eight of the top companies in the world offer their inside perspectives and career advice to students! These recruiters will shed light on the importance of the 7 Essentials and provide insights into how these essentials are utilized and beneficial within their respective companies. Most students receive

feedback from recruiters after interviewing with them, usually in the form of rejections when it's often too late! In Becoming The Best Me, students get advice from top company recruiters way before they start interviewing for jobs! And the type of advice received is focused more on career planning and preparation than on what to wear during interviews or what to put on a resume. The companies offering advice are **ACCENTURE, PRICEWATERHOUSECOOPERS, IBM, JEFFERSON PILOT, MICROSOFT, PEACE CORPS, ENTERPRISE RENT-A-CAR, & VERIZON.**

Nationwide Research on What Today's Employers are Looking For in Graduates

The 7 Career and Life Essentials featured in this book were not just "picked out of a hat." The author examined several research reports that, combined, surveyed thousands of company recruiters nationwide. The reports highlight those skills, personal qualities, experiences, and attitudes that are valued most by the hiring companies and their recruiters. Students won't just get one author's opinion on what recruiters are looking for – they will receive career advice "straight from the horse's mouth!"

Below are the four main areas of research used to generate the 7 Career & Life Essentials. I have included most of the major reports and graphs in the Appendix Section in the back of the book.

❶ Top New-Hire Skills and Personal Qualities (See Appendix A)
One of the best sources (if not the best) for identifying the skills and personal qualities valued by employers is the National Association of Colleges & Employers (NACE). The past four years of national employer surveys conducted by NACE, called *Job Outlook* surveys, were heavily used in generating the 7 Career & Life Essentials.

❷ Top Skills Wanted from Job Advertisements (See Appendix B)
A second source used to generate the Essentials comes from the Toronto Labor Market. The Human Resources Development Department tallies the core skills that employers requested in their job advertisements.

❸ Major Trends in the 21st Century Workplace (See Appendix C)
The third area of research examined current and future trends in the 21st century workplace. By looking at trends, it was possible to discover other essential qualities and skills needed to succeed in the new working world.

❹ Experiences Valued Most by Recruiters (See Appendix D)
A fourth area of research used to generate the 7 Essentials focused on the experiences in which students should participate in order to gain the essential skills and qualities.

In-Depth Descriptions of the 7 Career and Life Essentials
Becoming The Best Me features seven chapters, each revealing and describing one of the 7 *Career and Life Essentials*. The way that each Essential is thoroughly presented makes them come to life. Too often these key skills and qualities are presented in vague and generic ways. For example, students are frequently reminded of the importance of obtaining strong "people skills" (one of the 7 Essentials), yet are not taught the underlying qualities that make up a strong "people person." In this book, students will learn about the underlying qualities, attitudes, and characteristics of each Career and Life Essential.

Real-life Examples that "Hit Home"
The author uses many everyday-life examples that help students personally relate to the key concepts. For example, in the *Team Player* chapter, two unselfish softball players are used to illustrate the essence of teamwork.

Strategies on How to Acquire the 7 Essentials
Each chapter presents ways for students to begin developing the 7 Career and Life Essentials. Students will see that there are daily opportunities both in and out of the classroom to work on and ultimately develop the 7 Essentials.

e-portfolios
Appendix E introduces the concept of electronic portfolios (e-portfolios) and presents a 5-Step plan for students to produce their own e-portfolio. This appendix will be helpful to those teachers, counselors, and administrators who are attempting to incorporate e-portfolios in their respective schools.

Who Could Benefit from this Book?

Students
While the reading is more geared to middle school and high school students, elementary students could also indirectly benefit from this book. Elementary teachers and counselors could use the book to introduce the 7 Career and Life Essentials to their students and incorporate appropriate activities that facilitate the development of each Essential.

School-Work Administrators and Practitioners
Becoming The Best Me would be a perfect book around which to center K-12 Career Development Plans. For those schools that already have a solid K-12 Career Development Plan in place, this book would serve as a strong supplemental resource.

School Counselors
As elementary, middle school, and high school guidance counselors work individually with students, this book can be used to reinforce the importance of developing various skills, qualities, and attitudes in and out of the classroom.

Teachers
The 7 Career and Life Essentials are not only necessary to be an exceptional professional, but also to be an exceptional student and person. Teachers can use this book to enhance the teaching of the qualities and characteristics they're trying to instill in their students each and every day.

Parents

Parents recognize the importance of career preparation much more than their children do. Parents can use this book as a reminder of the skills, qualities, and attitudes that their children should strive to develop (at home and in school) in order to become a success in life.

School Counseling Graduate Programs and Colleges of Education

College and graduate students aspiring to become teachers and school counselors could use this book as a supplement to their textbooks. Receiving current perspectives from company recruiters across the country could add to their knowledge base related to students and their development as well as to career education programs.

Before You Begin...

One of the most important questions you'll need to answer in life is, "What do I want to be when I grow up?" You should continually explore careers and begin identifying those in which you're interested. **But what's even more important to answer right now in your life is, "What do I need to do in order to be successful in work AND in life?"** If you think about it, what's it really matter what career you choose if you're not going to be successful? And the reason you need to focus on this question NOW is that becoming successful doesn't happen when you're all grown up and out in the workforce; becoming successful is a process that starts early in your life and continues forever.

Simply put, nobody becomes great in a day. Do golfers hit par the first day they go golfing? Do artists paint their masterpieces the first time they pick up a brush? No! The best golfers and artists develop and sharpen their skills over a long period of time. It's common to hear a great golfer say, "I swung my first golf club before I could talk," or to hear a talented artist say, "I've been drawing for as long as I can remember."

Likewise, to *become the best you* in life, you have to start now. In this book, thousands of company recruiters nationwide indicate 7 essentials that make people successful in their careers (see the surveys in Appendix A, B, C, and D). All seven are things that you should be developing now in order to be successful in life and in any career you choose. We call these "things" *Career & Life Essentials*, for these 7 essentials which are sought after by recruiters are the same 7 attributes found in the most successful people, in both work and in life. Behind every great worker is a great person!

As you begin reading about the *7 Career & Life Essentials*, take special note of the underlying qualities of each essential and the strategies presented to help you acquire each. Once you clearly understand the 7 Essentials and their strategies, start thinking of ways for *you* to develop each of these underlying qualities and ultimately take ownership of the 7 Essentials.

Also take special note of all the direct quotes (presented throughout each chapter in 3-D boxes) that are offered by recruiters from eight of the best companies in America:

- **Accenture** (Consulting Firm)
- **Enterprise** (Car-Rental Company)
- **IBM** (Technology Firm)
- **Jefferson Pilot** (Insurance & Finance Company)
- **Microsoft** (Software Company)
- **Peace Corps** (Volunteer Service Organization)
- **PricewaterhouseCoopers** (Accounting Firm)
- **Verizon** (Telecommunications Company)

These top recruiters explain how the 7 Career & Life Essentials are valued and utilized within their respective companies. It's always good to get advice "straight from the horse's mouth!"

As you develop the 7 Essentials, you should strongly consider tracking these essential experiences and attributes in an electronic portfolio, better known as an *e-portfolio* (see Appendix E). We're in a "just do it and move on" society, racing from one experience to the next without taking time to reflect on what we learned and what skills we developed. Developing and maintaining an e-portfolio will enable you to take stock of your skills and accomplishments and successfully market yourself to college and company recruiters. Appendix E presents the ins and outs of developing your very own e-portfolio!

Finally, I hope you enjoy learning about the 7 Career & Life Essentials and making them a part of you. I've included many examples and stories that I think you'll relate to which will help bring key points to life and add a little entertainment value. It can actually be a lot of fun working towards *becoming the best you*!

BECOMING THE BEST ME

Chapter One

Career & Life Essential # 1
Be a PEOPLE PERSON

" Strong interpersonal skills are the cornerstone for being considered for almost every job at Microsoft. This starts in the interview process as soon as a candidate is contacted. If the candidate cannot interact effectively with recruiters, how will that person be effective in communicating with his/her manager, other employees and most importantly—the customer? "

—*Microsoft*

4

What Is A "People Person?"

A "People Person" is another (more informal) way to describe someone who has strong *interpersonal* skills. And a person with strong interpersonal skills is someone who is able to relate well with a wide variety of people and who loves to be with people.

What Is the Difference Between Interpersonal and Communication Skills?

Before we jump right in and start talking about the ins and outs of interpersonal skills, let's make sure we know what we mean when we say someone has strong interpersonal skills. A lot of people refer to "interpersonal" and "communication" skills interchangeably. After listening to a speaker, a member in the audience may say to her friend, "Boy, she really has strong interpersonal skills." Or, if someone gets along well with others, people tend to say, "He really communicates well with people."

> **"**Interpersonal skills come into play in a variety of ways, every day at Microsoft. Software design engineers must be able to interact effectively with their colleagues to complete projects, product managers must be able to communicate with senior management about product strategy and senior management needs to be able to sell their ideas for developing, marketing and selling products to their fellow senior leaders including Steve Ballmer and Bill Gates. **"**
>
> *—Microsoft*

So are they one and the same? If people are able to communicate well, do they naturally have strong interpersonal skills? Let's take a look at the following exchange between two high school friends, Addie and Olivia:

Olivia: *Addie, tell me what you think about the opening paragraph of my research paper. I put a lot of time into it; I need the opening to be strong.*

Addie: *The first sentence is written very poorly. The incorporation of adjectives used to describe the science author leaves much to be desired. I would seriously consider starting over.*

Olivia: *Just forget it! Sorry I bothered you!*

Did Addie verbally communicate her thoughts well? Communicating well means that you're able to articulate your thoughts clearly and fluently. Was it clear what Addie was trying to tell Olivia? I'd say it was crystal clear. Addie's communication skills were strong. How were her interpersonal skills? Having strong interpersonal skills has to do with how well you relate to others and how well your expressed thoughts and actions are received. **A big part of being interpersonal is having a level of sensitivity to others and expressing yourself tactfully**.

Was Addie very tactful when giving feedback to Olivia? Not really. Was she sensitive to the fact that Olivia put a lot of time in writing this opening paragraph? No, she wasn't. So, in this scenario, it is pretty safe to say that Addie demonstrated strong communication skills and weak interpersonal skills. Take a look at a different exchange that occurred between Addie and Olivia:

> **Olivia**: *Addie, tell me what you think about the opening paragraph of my research paper. I put a lot of time into it; I need the opening to be strong.*

> **Addie**: *Well, like, the first sentence, was, like, good – don't get me wrong, but, um, it maybe could use a tad more enthusiasm. Um, also, like, I really liked overall how you, um, were, trying to like describe that author guy. But, um, I don't know, I think maybe we could think of a different word to describe him than, like, awesome.*

> **Olivia**: *Thanks a lot Addie. I'll get right on that!*

How would you rate Addie this time around? How well did she communicate her thoughts? Was she articulate, clear, and fluent? No. Certainly, few people would say Addie possessed strong communication skills in this recent scenario. But how were her interpersonal skills? Was Addie a little more sensitive towards Olivia? Absolutely. Don't you think that Olivia would receive Addie's feedback less defensively this second time around? Therefore, during this second scenario, Addie demonstrated stronger interpersonal skills than she did before, but her communication skills were much weaker. So, it IS possible to have very strong communication skills and very poor interpersonal skills, and vice versa.

As the scenarios above illustrated, tactfulness and sensitivity are basic interpersonal skills. But there is more to it. In the next part of this chapter, we're going to describe several qualities that enable someone to have strong interpersonal skills – in other words, to be a People Person.

Identifying and Developing the Qualities of a People Person

It's not enough for you to say, "I want to become a people person" or "I want to develop my interpersonal skills." Just how would you develop your interpersonal skills? Beneath strong interpersonal skills are a number of personal qualities. The trick is to understand what these qualities are, and then work on making them a part of you. Below are descriptions of six key qualities of a People Person, as well as some pointers on how you can develop these qualities. Acquiring these strong qualities is very important to the development of strong interpersonal skills.

1. Awareness/Conscientiousness

Remember that a fundamental aspect of being a People Person is *being able to relate well with others*. In order to relate well with others, you must be aware of other people and their feelings. Some people refer to this quality as having "street sense." Someone who has good street sense has a good feel or understanding of his or her surroundings. You can sense what is going on and therefore anticipate others' actions. For example, if you have good street sense, you will be able to anticipate a fight or sense a bad situation coming on. You will know when someone is down and take action to help that person feel better. Being conscientious is thinking through and caring about the consequences of your actions. Thus, in order to relate well with others, you must always be aware of people's states of mind and feelings, and be conscientious (careful) in what you say and how you act around them.

> "Our company's mission is to provide our customers with exceptional service and to provide our employees with ample training and opportunities to build successful careers. One large part of fulfilling this mission is being able to understand our customers and their needs."
>
> —*Enterprise Rent-A-Car*

2. Diplomacy/Tactfulness

Being diplomatic or tactful goes hand in hand with being aware and conscientious. This quality, however, focuses more on your actions than on your thoughts or gut instincts. Being aware of the feelings of others enables you to act diplomatically or tactfully. Let's examine a couple of scenarios to better understand diplomacy and tact:

Zach and Andrew are members of the Politics Club at their school. Various club members are engaged in a debate about raising taxes. Andrew believes in raising taxes, and Zach is against it. After Andrew gives his argument for raising taxes, Zach replies:

Obviously, Andrew has no idea what he's talking about. Hey, Andrew, when you make an argument, it helps to actually know something about the subject. People who think that raising taxes is the answer don't have a clue!

> "Strong interpersonal skills and the ability to adapt in conversation will allow individuals to remain resilient in the following situations: conversing with ease, negotiating, handling criticism, coaching someone to improve performance, and expressing dissatisfaction effectively."
>
> –*Verizon*

Behaving tactfully means that you will choose your words wisely so that you do not offend or embarrass someone. Was Zach diplomatic or tactful in this situation? Not at all. And would you say that this lack of diplomacy will hurt his chances of relating well with Andrew and others who are on Andrew's side? Let's look at a more tactful Zach.

I understand where Andrew is coming from. His point on raising taxes for the benefit of children makes some sense. However, I believe that there is a broader issue that we should be considering.

You see, being tactful doesn't mean that you have no backbone and that you have to agree with everyone all the time. You CAN DISAGREE with others and stand up for what you believe in WITHOUT OFFENDING others. It is all in how you package your argument. Don't be afraid to disagree or confront someone, just do it tactfully. And remember, sometimes doing it tactfully means that you have to calm yourself down before you respond to someone. It's hard being tactful when your emotions get the best of you. Take a deep breath or two, be aware of who you're talking to, think about what you'd like to say, and go for it. You will learn much more about dealing with conflicts and confronting others in Chapter Three.

> **"**Any interaction with a client requires solid interpersonal skills. Whether in a presentation, negotiation, or discussion, Accenture personnel build rapport by engaging others in a congenial and professional way.**"**
> —*Accenture*

3. Ability to Actively Listen

One of the most underrated personal qualities is being a good listener. Stop and think for a minute about the people that you know who are good listeners. Don't you love them? In this hustle and bustle world, it's a treat to have someone who really listens to you. What a gift to give to others when you're able to put all the stuff that is going on in your life aside and actively listen to them! There is simply no better interpersonal quality to have than to give of yourself and really be there for someone who needs it. You may think that you are fooling people into thinking that you're listening, but most people can tell when you're not. Here's an example of a poor listener:

Dave: *Hey Art, how's it going?*
Art: *Not so good.*
Dave: *Cool.*
Art: *Hey Dave, you got a minute?*
Dave: *Sure.*
Art: *Man, I might have blown my chances of getting into college. I think I may get a "C" in Pre-Calculus.*
Dave: *Ah, don't let it bother you. Hey, are you going to the concert on Friday? How did you get your ticket?*

Was Dave *actively* listening to Art? Was he able to put his issues aside and really be there for Art? Dave started off by asking how Art was doing, and he responded "cool" when Art said, "Not so good." Is Dave someone you would call a people person? A people person is someone you like to be around. It's not much fun being around someone who doesn't listen to you. Let's give Dave another shot. The following is an example of "Active Listening Dave."

> **Dave**: *Hey Art, how's it going?*
>
> **Art**: *Not so good.*
>
> **Dave**: *Really? What's up?*
>
> **Art**: *Man, I might have blown my chances of getting into college. I think I may get a "C" in Pre-Calculus.*
>
> **Dave**: *Are you serious? Darn it. Why do you think you may get a "C"?*

Now Dave is being an active listener. One of the best ways to show that you are listening actively to someone is by asking follow-up questions. None of us wants to bore people with our problems, but when people give you the green light by asking follow-up questions, it sure is nice! This may all seem elementary, but when you have a thousand things on your mind as most people do, it's difficult to be unselfish and actively listen.

> **"**Interpersonal skills are critical in team environments. In a dynamically changing corporate environment, employees must remain strong and rely on the power of strong communication, which includes communication through listening as well as through dialogue.**"**
> **—*Verizon***

The best way to become more of an active listener (if you're not already) is to be "aware" of your natural tendency to drift off or lose focus when people are talking to you. When you start to "consciously" catch yourself not really listening, you can begin to change this habit by learning to put your concerns away for a while and listen. You will be surprised how good you feel about yourself when you do this.

> **"**Our consultants conduct information-gathering interviews with our clients' employees to understand the "as-is" state of a particular business process. At times, our client's employees may feel anxious about sharing information [talking and listening] with outsiders. It is critical that our consultants use their strong interpersonal skills to gain the trust of these employees so that they can gather the information needed for the analysis.**"**
> **—*PricewaterhouseCoopers***

4. Open-Mindedness

Once again, being able to relate well with others is at the essence of interpersonal skills. However, what's key in an increasingly diverse world and workforce is relating well with a wide-variety of people from diverse cultures and backgrounds. The only way to do this is to be open-minded. You have learned by now that not everyone looks like you, thinks like you, acts like you, or believes everything you believe. A key to being open-minded and ultimately *becoming the best you* is accepting the fact that there is not one right way of doing things or one right way of being. Open-minded people are intrigued by differences in others rather than frustrated that others are not more like them. You don't have to like everyone, but you should always respect their differences. In the next chapter, we will go into much greater depth about being open to differences and truly appreciating diversity. For now, just remember that it is an oxymoron to say that someone who does not appreciate diversity is a People Person!

5. Humility (Humble)

People naturally like others who are humble. Very few people like those who brag about themselves. Think how you feel about someone who boastfully tells you he got an "A" on a paper versus someone who didn't tell you he got an "A" until you asked him, and then tells you he got lucky. Don't you feel better about yourself when you keep your successes to yourself, and only reveal them when people ask or take note?

> "Accenture works with clients to solve their business issues and provide solutions for their continued success. We seek individuals who possess strong interpersonal skills because they will be working closely with Accenture and client teams while working toward a common goal."
>
> —*Accenture*

Part of being humble is being unselfish. Can you think of people you know who always are talking about themselves?

"Hey, guess what happened to me?"
"You guys, I am so happy. I aced the test today."
"You should have seen me last night. I played better than I ever have."

When you are at a party or just hanging out with friends, the unselfish thing to do is to ask others how they are doing.

"Hey Julie, how's your day been?"
"What's up Bo? How'd you do on that test you were studying for?"
"Rocky, how'd you do last night? Did you win your match?"

A selfish person will always initiate things about himself or herself. A People Person will ask others about their lives.

6. Good Sense of Humor

How many times have you heard someone say, "I really like her; she's so funny." Or, "He has a good sense of humor; he's a great guy." People like others who have a sense of humor. It's fun to be around someone who makes you laugh. We live in a fast-paced, dog-eat-dog world. Isn't it nice to take a break occasionally and have a good laugh?

If you want to develop a good sense of humor, don't go out and buy a joke book and force jokes on everyone. The best way to develop your sense of humor is to relax, be yourself, and don't take everything so seriously. It's healthy to be able to laugh at yourself. You're not going to be perfect every day of your life. Everyone has a bloopers highlight video—but not everyone is secure enough to share it with others. Remember to keep things in perspective, lighten your stress load, and laugh occasionally.

> **"**Interpersonal skills are another way to describe being able to sell yourself. Whether you're with a client or working on a global project you will need to have self confidence, a positive attitude, maturity, be a team player, fluency of expression (non-verbal many times being very important outside the US), and humor.**"**
>
> —*IBM*

How to become more of a People Person

The first step in becoming a People Person and developing strong interpersonal skills is to understand and value the six underlying personal qualities presented above. The second step is to take an honest look at yourself and determine which of these qualities you already possess, and which ones you need to develop. Ask people who know you best to give you honest feedback regarding how these qualities apply to you. This second step is very important. You know what they say: "Once you admit to something, you're halfway there!"

Once this is done, it's time for you to get out there and mix it up with people. But this time, as you interact with others, try to incorporate as many of these qualities as you can. Whether you're in class, at practice, or just hanging out with your friends, try your best to be a positive People Person! For example, when you're talking with someone, try extra-hard to actively listen to them. When you disagree with someone, state why you disagree in a tactful way. Look for the good things in people and compliment them on those things rather than pointing out the bad. Ask people about their day before telling them all about you and your day. In other words, take these six interpersonal characteristics out on the road with you as you carry out your typical day.

Finally, make it a habit to analyze your various interactions with people at the end of each day. Reflect on the qualities that you carried out well, and with which those you struggled. Think about what you could have done differently to be more effective interpersonally. The more you reflect, the more you'll be able to develop those interpersonal qualities that need the most work. It's important to realize that every single person has the potential of becoming a People Person, but for some it takes more effort. It takes more than just learning about the six underlying qualities – you have to be committed to making them qualities of your own!

Why Company Recruiters put Interpersonal Skills at the top of their Wish List

With all the excitement centered on modern technology and the importance of having computer skills, you might think that computer skills would be on the top of recruiters' wish lists. Or due to the importance of solving new problems and life-long learning, wouldn't analytical skills be most important? It turns out that over the past half-decade, interpersonal skills have been on the top of the wish lists of most recruiters. Why?

> " It is important that our company hires graduates that possess strong interpersonal skills, because doing the specific job is only part of the overall skill of doing the entire job. Being able to relate with other individuals is more than 50% of what's needed to be a great employee."
>
> *—Jefferson Pilot*

When recruiters are asked, "Why are interpersonal skills more important than some of the other key skills," most give an answer similar to the one below.

When we need employees to learn a new computer application, we can train them on that. If employees need to brush up on their communication skills, there are plenty of communication seminars out there to send them to. However, if employees come to us without good interpersonal skills, it takes much more than trying to enhance a skill or two; it's trying to change the type of person that they are! For example, how do you train an insensitive person to become more sensitive when confronting others? How can we train someone to be more positive if he or she is naturally a more negative person? How do we get people who bring 20 years worth of stereotypes with them to appreciate diversity?

Remember, good interpersonal skills incorporate a host of personal qualities that have been presented in this chapter. Training someone to have stronger interpersonal skills means that you have to change many personal qualities that make up that person.

> " As a consulting organization, we are in the business of providing clients with advice, guidance, and solutions that will transform and enhance the way they do business. All of our consultants, no matter their level, will be constantly interacting with clients. Strong Interpersonal Skills are critical to the establishment, development and nurturing of client relationships. "
>
> —*PricewaterhouseCoopers*

Besides the difficulty of helping a person become a People Person, there is another main reason interpersonal skills are so valued by recruiters: these skills greatly affect the chemistry and morale within companies. Someone's negative interpersonal skills can have a negative impact on many of the employees around him. Conversely, an employee who has strong interpersonal skills can have a positive influence on others and help make the work atmosphere more pleasant. Remember, interpersonal skills are contagious!

The Whole In One

* The recruiters offer their own insights on the positive effects of interpersonal skills.

* Interpersonal Skills and Communication Skills are definitely not the same. You can have one without the other.

* There are six qualities that enable one to possess strong interpersonal skills:
   1. Awareness/Conscientiousness
   2. Diplomacy/Tactfulness
   3. Ability to Actively Listen
   4. Open Mindedness
   5. Humility (Humble)
   6. Good Sense of Humor

* Recruiters place interpersonal skills at the top of their wish lists because they are much harder to develop, and because they have a big impact on the morale of a team.

BECOME THE BEST YOU ...BE A PEOPLE PERSON!

Chapter Two

Career & Life Essential # 2, Be a Person Who
APPRECIATES DIVERSITY

"When you look at the country and the changing face of the population, it becomes clear that having a diverse workforce and supplier network is not just a good idea, but an essential one. It is a goal at Enterprise to have our workforce mirror the communities in which we do business, and all of our employees need to understand the importance of having a company that supports and respects all people. In short, we strive to ensure that our company is inclusive and supportive of people of all backgrounds."

—Enterprise Rent-A-Car

Defining the Phrase "Appreciating Diversity"

A person who really appreciates diversity realizes the many benefits it brings to a team, group, or community. It's important, however, to clarify what we mean when we say "appreciate diversity." First of all, what do we mean by "diversity?" Diversity is another way of saying "differences" or "variations." Most of us think of racial differences when we hear the term diversity. However, there are many other types of diversity. Below are some examples of types of diversity found in the workplace and in life:

- Ethnic/Racial: African-American, Asian-American, Caucasian, Hispanic-American, Native American, etc.
- Gender: female, male
- Disability Status: visually impaired, hearing impaired, paralyzed, etc.
- Citizenship: U.S citizen, foreign national, international student, etc.
- Sexual Orientation: heterosexual, homosexual, bisexual, etc.
- Religious Affiliation: Catholic, Jewish, Muslim, Protestant, etc.
- Marital & Family Status: married, single, divorced, single parent, etc.
- Socioeconomic Status: wealthy, poor, unemployed, on welfare, etc.
- Geographic/Regional: southerners, New Englanders, etc.
- Height and weight: tall, short, skinny, overweight, etc.
- Hair color: blond, red-head, brunette, etc.
- Personality: funny, shy, outgoing, etc.
- Intelligence: smart, stupid, nerdy, etc.
- Work ethic: lazy, hard-working, etc.

> " It is important for us to hire people that possess an appreciation of diversity because people of different backgrounds, socially, economically, ethnically are people that provide a pool of creative ideas and resources that the entire team can draw from."
>
> *—Jefferson Pilot*

This list, while not all-inclusive, should give you an idea of how many different types of diversity there are. It's important that you broaden your concept of diversity and think about the many ways people are different from you and from one another.

We also need to understand what the word "appreciate" means in the phrase "appreciate diversity." Looking at the difference between appreciating diversity and tolerating diversity can help us better understand what this is all about.

Appreciating Diversity vs. Tolerating Diversity

> **"** A good example of when an appreciation of diversity benefits Microsoft is how the company continues to develop products that have functionality for persons with disabilities. One out of five Americans (according to NOD), and therefore, one out of five customers, has a disability. Through an appreciation for diversity, Microsoft recognizes that information technology is one of the most important enabling factors for persons with disabilities in the workplace.**"**
>
> *—Microsoft*

Unfortunately, there are too many people in this world who only tolerate diversity. When someone tolerates diversity, they don't really believe in the benefits of diversity. They keep their real feelings and biases to themselves and go through the motions because they feel it's something they have to accept. Let me give you an example:

The Tolerating Banker

Joe, a white male, works at a bank. Joe comes from a small, rural town, where there were hardly any racial minority members. In his town growing up, it was common to tell racist jokes and to put down people from different races and cultures. Thus, overall, Joe had developed a bias against racial minority people. However, as part of the training program at his bank, Joe learned about the bank's philosophy of being open and appreciating people from all cultures and backgrounds. It was clear that an employee could be fired if this philosophy is not upheld. Recently, the bank hired an Asian-American teller, Greg. Joe was not happy about this, and he felt uncomfortable talking to Greg. One day, Greg asked Joe if he would make a photocopy for him. Joe didn't like taking orders from Greg, but he did it anyway. Joe resents Greg for asking him to do this and now tries to avoid him as much as possible.

I wish I could say this never happens anymore. However, this kind of passive racism still exists. Joe clearly does not appreciate Greg and the ways in which he can make positive contributions to the bank, but he is willing to keep his mouth shut so he doesn't get fired. In other words, Joe merely tolerates Greg in order to keep his job.

When you appreciate diversity, you respect the differences in others and appreciate the added value that these differences can bring. To become the best you, you must make a strong effort to learn how to appreciate diversity!

> "Diversity at Accenture is a top priority because solutions to complex business problems are best solved by people with different backgrounds. Accenture fosters an environment rich in diversity that acknowledges each individual's uniqueness, values his or her skills and contributions and promotes respect, personal achievement and stewardship. "Respect for the individual" is one of our core values, and we strive to build an inclusive environment in which all employees feel valued and appreciated."
>
> —*Accenture*

> "From the Peace Corps' very beginning, people of color have brought their spirit of service and altruism to help communities in developing countries overcome the challenges they face. And they have brought that same spirit back to communities across our own country, helping America respond to its own challenges. This is why the Peace Corps actively recruits people from all backgrounds, including African Americans, Hispanic Americans, Asian Americans, Native Americans, and people from other racial, ethnic, and religious backgrounds who are so important to our country's past and its future."
>
> —*Peace Corps*

Learning to Appreciate Diversity

Talking about diversity, especially regarding race, gender, and sexual orientation, is a sensitive subject for many people. The delicate nature of diversity keeps us from dealing with it more openly. However, with the workplace and our world becoming increasingly more diverse, it is imperative that you take the steps necessary to develop your appreciation of and belief in diversity. People need to take a good hard look at themselves regarding their thoughts and feelings about diversity issues.

Follow the Three-Step Plan

The following is a three-step plan to further develop your appreciation of diversity:

Step One: Own Up To Your Biases and Prejudices

People are embarrassed to admit that they have biases and prejudices toward certain groups of people. The term "prejudiced" is especially harsh for most people. To say that someone is prejudiced implies that that person is a bad person. Our natural instinct is to defend ourselves, so we deny having any biases or prejudices. And, since "we are not prejudiced," we don't have to deal with the issue, right?

The first step that we all have to take is to stop thinking of prejudice and bias as a huge stigma, because if we continue to think of it in this way, we will continue to deny our biases and fail to do anything about them.

We all have biases – accept it and move on!

We were all born and raised in different towns and cities, some of which had a great deal of diversity, others that had very little. Parents, grandparents, sisters and brothers, uncles and aunts, cousins, friends, teachers, coaches, and many other people have influenced us all. We all are part of a certain ethnic and racial culture and have varying religious beliefs. Because of all of these influences and associations, there is no way that you could not have developed some emotional leanings toward a certain side. If you never had the opportunity to interact with certain groups of people, how could you possibly avoid having preconceived opinions about these groups of people?

> "Our current and future business is based on our ability to respect and embrace many different cultures. Our employees need to have the same appreciation for the benefits of embracing and working with people who come from many different backgrounds and bring different experiences to the table. Respecting diversity is the only way an organization can be successful long-term in the global economy."
>
> *—Pricewaterhouse Coopers*

It's time for people to stop beating themselves up for having biases and prejudices. Only then will you be able to more openly explore and challenge your biases. The thoughts and feelings that you have toward certain groups of people do exist. It's ok that you have them. However, it is **not** ok to deny them and to do nothing about them!

Step Two: Catch Yourself and Identify Your Biases and Prejudices
Admitting that you have biases is a big part of the battle. The next step is to be aware of the biases and prejudices that you have and learn to catch yourself when you have these thoughts and feelings. If you cannot identify your biases and prejudices, how can you ever explore and question them? Consider the following example.

Pat, a high school student in Connecticut, is taking a marketing class. A big part of the class was to complete a semester-long team project. The teacher was pairing off students in teams of two. Pat was hoping to be teamed up with a good student who would carry his or her weight. The teacher assigned Jennifer to work with Pat. Jennifer's family recently moved from Georgia to Connecticut and she had a thick, southern accent. Because he was from the

North, Pat had a bias in favor of northerners who he believed worked quickly and completed tasks efficiently and effectively. He stereotypes southerners as people who move at a slow pace and are a little flighty. Pat had a preconceived opinion of Jennifer.

Now, if Pat isn't acutely aware of this prejudice, he'll probably treat Jennifer with little respect and think that he has to do all the work to get an "A." However, if Pat is able to catch himself and admit that he is being biased, he may give Jennifer a chance.

Step Three: Challenge Your Biases and Give Everyone a Chance

As you catch yourself and identify your biases, you need to *challenge* the bias or prejudice that is staring you in the face and give the person with whom you are interacting a chance. Give all people the respect they deserve by treating them like unique human beings. I want to share with you a story I once heard from an African American speaker that emphasizes the importance of giving people a chance:

"Last week I had a long flight across the country. As I got on the plane, I noticed that my seat was right next to this big country-looking guy! I mean, he was all dressed up like a cowboy, with his cowboy hat, and cowboy shirt, tight pants, and cowboy boots. My first instinct was to think, 'Man, why me! Why do I have to sit next to this red-neck all trip long? Well, I'm not gonna talk to this idiot!' But then, I caught myself! Even though he looked like a red-neck, I challenged myself to be a big person and not write this guy off. So, I started a conversation by introducing myself. Well, we weren't like best friends or anything, but we talked once in a while during this long trip, and he wasn't all that bad. And most importantly, I felt pretty good about going against my natural instinct to write him off! If each of you would just do that, the world would be a much better place!"

What a great message! When you start feeling negative toward certain people, don't just write them off; challenge that feeling (bias) and give them a chance! You should also remember that you CAN influence and control your feelings and emotions. Keeping an open mind and thinking positively can *feed* your heart in a healthy way:

An Old Indian Grandfather

An old Indian Grandfather said to his grandson who came to him with anger at a friend who had done him an injustice........

"Let me tell you a story. I too, at times, have felt a great hate for those that have taken so much, with no sorrow for what they do. But hate wears you down, and does not hurt your enemy. It is like taking poison and wishing your enemy would die. I have struggled with these feelings many times."

He continued......

"It is as if there are two wolves inside me;

One is good and does no harm. He lives in harmony with all around him and does not take offense when no offense was intended. He will only fight when it is right to do so, and in the right way. He saves all his energy for the right fight.

But the other wolf, ahhh!

He is full of anger. The littlest thing will set him into a fit of temper. He fights everyone, all the time, for no reason. He cannot think because his anger and hate are so great. It is helpless anger, for his anger will change nothing.

Sometimes it is hard to live with these two wolves inside me, for both of them try to dominate my spirit."

The boy looked intently into his Grandfather's eyes and asked...

"Which one wins, Grandfather?"

The Grandfather smiled and quietly said......

"The one I feed."

—*Indian Author Unknown*

We all need to feed the positive feelings and thoughts we have toward others rather than the petty negative ones.

Get Involved in Multicultural Experiences

Diversity is all around you. You have an opportunity every day to interact with people from different backgrounds, cultures, and orientations. Challenge yourself and get to know a wide variety of people. Also, make sure you take full advantage of the plethora of multicultural experiences that are available. The following are opportunities you might encounter that will help you to develop your appreciation for diversity.

Study a Foreign Language

Many countries require children to learn to speak more than one language. Unfortunately, the United States is not one of them. Even though lately there has been a greater push to learn how to speak Spanish, as a nation we don't emphasize the importance of being bilingual as much as we should. However, there are plenty of opportunities in school to learn how to speak a second language. Most schools offer courses on speaking, reading and writing a foreign language.

"Volunteers live in communities overseas where English is not the primary language that is spoken. Thus, there is a need to learn a new language. In addition, not only does a volunteer need to learn a new language, they must be able to communicate with host country nationals to succeed in the goals of their projects."

—*Peace Corps*

Use the wonderful resources that you have at your fingertips to learn a different language. There will be no other time in your life that you will have this convenient of an opportunity to do so. Take advantage of it now! Later, if you go to college, you can even major or minor in a foreign language and culture. French and Spanish are two traditional majors. Foreign language study opens doors to understanding and appreciating other cultures.

Take a Multi-cultural/Race-Relations Course

Many schools offer at least one course on diversity, usually called Multicultural Issues, Race Relations, or Ethnic and Racial Diversity. During the class, you will learn about different cultures and about people with different orientations and religious beliefs. You'll learn about the barriers that prevent people from getting along and the key factors of integration. You may even have a chance to engage in open dialogue with classmates that come from different races and backgrounds. You'll also learn a lot about yourself and your own biases and prejudices.

> **"** In today's global marketplace, it is important for your workforce to be a reflection of your customers. IBM has a strong history of working with many international, national and regional diversity groups on the professional and university level.**"**
>
> *—IBM*

Study or Travel Abroad

Traveling to a different country is a wonderful way to develop your appreciation of diversity. You should also look into opportunities for studying abroad. Talk to your guidance counselor about the possibility of becoming an exchange student for a semester or year. Usually you will be able to choose from among several different countries. While you are there, make sure you soak in the culture and get to know the locals. Learn about the prevalent religion(s), customs, norms, and values. Spend as much time as you can with people from different cultures. It's tempting to just hang out with your family or, if studying abroad, with fellow students from your own country, but you'll be missing out on half of the learning experience if you don't get out there and meet different people. Remember to be aware of your biases and to challenge your preconceived opinions as you meet people who are different from you.

> **"** Our company has clients in a multitude of industries that operate in multiple countries around the world. When our employees appreciate and understand those cultural differences, we can more easily deploy them to support those clients both here in the United States and abroad.**"**
>
> *—PricewaterhouseCoopers*

As a career counselor and advisor, I have found that when students consider studying abroad, they are often apprehensive about leaving their homeland and living in a new country and culture. It's always fun to see the big smile on their faces when they return. The students always come back saying that it was the best experience of their lives, and that it has changed their perspectives on life. Don't miss out on this life-changing opportunity if you get the chance to study abroad!

Rent the movie *Remember the Titans*

There are a number of movies and videos out there that center on racism and diversity. However, one of the more recent ones that should be seen by every high school student is *Remember the Titans*, starring Denzel Washington. This movie effectively delivers the message that when students from a different race are forced to spend quality time together, they eventually get to know and appreciate the person underneath the skin color.

You Can Make a Difference

You can make a difference. Your attitude and actions can have a profound effect upon those around you. There is no better example of this than the story of Rosa Parks. In Montgomery, Alabama, in December 1955, Parks boarded a bus after a long day of work. She was tired, and so she took an open seat. The bus grew more crowded and Parks, an African-American woman, was ordered to give up her seat to a white woman. She refused and the white bus driver threatened to have her arrested. She refused again to move and was arrested. Because of her arrest, the entire African-American population of Montgomery boycotted the buses. Within a year, Montgomery's public transportation system was legally integrated. One of the most significant moments of the civil rights movement occurred because of one woman who refused to go to the back of the bus! You, too, can make a difference by setting an example to all those around you when you take positive steps toward being a person who appreciates diversity.

The Whole in One

- Appreciation of diversity should be a goal for all of us. It's not enough to simply tolerate diversity.

- Diversity is not just drawn along racial lines. There are issues of diversity in gender, sexual orientation, citizenship, marital status, religious affiliation, and many other areas.

- In order to develop an appreciation of diversity, biases and prejudices must be owned up to, caught, and challenged and everyone must be given the benefit of the doubt.

- There are many diversity and multicultural opportunities:
    1. Learn a foreign language
    2. Take a course in cultural diversity
    3. Travel or study abroad
    4. Rent *Remember The Titans*

- YOU can make a difference!

BECOME THE BEST YOU ...BE A PERSON WHO APPRECIATES DIVERSITY!

Chapter Three

Career & Life Essential # 3
Be a TEAM PLAYER

"Lou Gerstner, Chairman and CEO of IBM, said, "Integration is superior to Isolation." I've used this philosophy many times while speaking with students seeking full-time jobs or internships (It's also at the bottom of all my emails). It doesn't matter if you are a Technician or a Public Relations Specialist—defining a process or delivering a solution—a Team Project will be part of your career development. New employees that already embrace the concept of being a team player (there is no "I" in team) will find that projects can be challenging and fun rather than frustrating and disruptive."

—IBM

Being a Team Player

If you are going to develop into the best you, being a team player is very important. To help us identify the essential qualities necessary to be team player, let's take a look at a definition from the *New Webster's Dictionary and Thesaurus*:

Teamwork: The quality whereby individuals unselfishly subordinate their own part to the general effort of the group with whom they are working or playing.

As we look at the definition of "teamwork," the key terms and phrases that stand out are *unselfish, subordinate their own part*, and *general effort of the group*. An essential quality of a good team is the ability to *work together* effectively towards a common goal. Another key quality is that the members of the team *believe in a common purpose or goal.*

Thus, using the key phrases and terms from the definition, here are four key qualities of a team player:

❶ Believes in the common goal of the team

❷ Works effectively together with other team members

❸ Is unselfish

❹ Subordinates his or her own part or self interests for the betterment of the team

> " Accenture seeks people who are team players because project team members must work together to achieve common goals for their clients. Being a good team player and sharing with colleagues contributes to the overall success of the project. We do not encourage people working on their own in silos, but rather a collaborative environment where workload, ideas and solutions can be shared."
>
> *—Accenture*

Analyzing athletic teams has always been a good way to clearly see good teamwork in effect, since the *common purpose or goal* is easy to see: Winning. Look at the following example that is based on a situation that actually occurred:

Missy and Alicia are two stars on their high school softball team. As seniors, they are playing the last game of their high school career today—the conference championship. Missy is an all-star shortstop who is one double play shy of the all-time conference record. Alicia is just three hits short of the team record for most hits in a season. The team they are playing against in the conference championship is famous for hitting the long ball, especially to left field. Unfortunately, the left fielder for the Greyhounds has a sprained knee and cannot play in the big game. Therefore, the coach approaches Missy and asks her to consider something: "Missy, I hate asking you to consider this, but our best chance of winning is to have you out in left field. This would blow your chance of getting the double-play record, but we need a strong arm in left field to win. I would completely understand if you want to stay at shortstop. It's your call." Missy thinks it over, but doesn't need much time. She has always put the team first. She informs the coach that she would be playing in left field during the championship game.

Missy unselfishly subordinated her self-interest of getting the individual record, because she believed in the common goal of the team: winning the championship.

The game was tight. It was 4-4 in the last inning, and the Greyhounds had a base runner on second base. Alicia was up to bat. She had already gotten two hits—just one shy of the record for most hits in a season. There were no outs, so the best thing to do would have been to advance the runner on second base to third base. This would allow the next batter to just have to hit a fly ball to get the base runner to score the winning run. The other team's infield was playing way back, knowing that Alicia usually hits the ball hard. Alicia knew that she could easily bunt the ball and advance the runner to third, but she would likely get out and not get her third hit. Alicia surprised everyone and bunted the ball. The pitcher got the ball and threw Alicia out at first, but the runner on second advanced to third. The next batter got a hit and the Greyhounds won the championship.

Both Missy and Alicia understood what it meant to be team players. They sacrificed their own individual achievements for the team's common goal. You've probably heard the saying, "There is no 'I' in *Team.*" It is becoming increasingly common in the workplace to be assigned to a team to complete various projects. In your career and in life, a big part of your success, then, will depend on how well you work within teams, or how good of a team player you are. Additionally, you will remember from the previous chapter that the workplace is getting more diverse, so you must be able to work effectively with team members of different cultures and backgrounds.

> "We deliver all of our services to our clients through the hard work of our teams. Teams are a critical part of our culture because we believe that teamwork drives excellence in our concepts and deliverables to our clients. Teams help to create environments where new thoughts and ideas are stimulated and embraced. Teams will work together to produce results that will take our client's business to the next level. Teams are able to support and drive each other to grow and develop."
> —*PricewaterhouseCoopers*

How to Become a Team Player

Use Your Interpersonal Skills in Teams

To be a good team player, you have to be unselfish and willing to sacrifice yourself at times for the benefit of the team. In addition to these core team qualities, you obviously need to be able to relate well with your other team members. In other words, you must utilize the six underlying qualities of interpersonal skills presented in Chapter One. That's the reason why *People Person* (interpersonal skills) was the first Career & Life Essential presented in this book. Interpersonal skills are needed almost everywhere. Good interpersonal skills are necessary to work well with a wide variety of people (as seen in Chapter Two) and to work well in teams. You will not be a good team player if you don't work constantly on your interpersonal skills.

> " Individual contributors are an integral part of the company's make-up, but those individuals can be a part of many teams even if they have no reporting personnel. In other words, team players understand the impact of their work across the organization and the company. They do not work in a vacuum; their efforts are vertically integrated/streamlined into overarching company goals."
>
> —*Verizon*

Learn to Resolve Conflicts Effectively

When you are part of a team for a substantial period, it's almost inevitable that conflicts between members will occur. Someone does something you feel is wrong or hurtful to the goal of the team. What do you do? Remain quiet so as not to "make waves?" Not if you are a team player. One of the most important qualities of a team player is the ability to confront others tactfully. Following are three steps that can help you turn confrontations into a positive outcome.

Step 1: Have the Courage to Confront

Too often people choose to avoid confrontation. It's not easy to confront someone; nobody likes friction in a group. However, when people don't confront one another, frustration with others often turns to resentment and people start talking behind the backs of others. Ultimately, the team begins to splinter. Remember, a core quality of teamwork is to sacrifice your own self-interests for the benefit of the team. When you choose to avoid confrontation, you are keeping your own self-interests in mind—you don't want someone else to be mad at you. But by doing this, you're also disrespecting the person by talking behind his or her back and hurting the team in the process! Thus, the first step of confronting is to have enough "guts" to confront!

Step 2: Know WHERE and WHEN to Confront

The next step is to think about the most effective time and place to confront. If you have an issue with one person, it's usually best to approach that person individually. When you confront a person in front of a group, the person will naturally feel embarrassed and get defensive. You are putting that person on the spot and making other team members feel awkward. As for *when* to confront, don't do it if you are emotionally upset. It's best to give yourself time to cool down, think through what you want to say, and approach him or her later.

Step 3: Know HOW to Confront

When you do confront a team member, you want to do it as tactfully as you can. There is no benefit to belittling or offending him or her. You should think about what you want to say and choose your words wisely. Remember, the effects of hitting someone below the belt with a comment can last a very long time, as seen in the following story.

The Fence

There once was a little boy who had a bad temper. His father gave him a bag of nails and told him that every time he lost his temper, he must hammer a nail into the back of the fence.

The first day the boy had driven 37 nails into the fence. Over the next few weeks, as he learned to control his anger, the number of nails hammered daily gradually dwindled down. He discovered it was easier to hold his temper than to drive those nails into the fence.

Finally the day came when the boy didn't lose his temper at all. He told his father about it and the father suggested that the boy now pull out one nail for each day that he was able to hold his temper.

The days passed and the young boy was finally able to tell his father that all the nails were gone. The father took his son by the hand and led him to the fence. He said, "You have done well, my son, but look at the holes in the fence. The fence will never be the same. When you say things in anger, they leave a scar just like this one. You can put a knife in a man and draw it out. It won't matter how many times you say I'm sorry, the wound is still there. A verbal wound is as bad as a physical one."

—Author Unknown

Remember this story if you are one who speaks before thinking, especially if what you say could be hurtful. The way the conflict is resolved – and therefore the stability of the team – may depend largely on the way you approach the issue.

Examples of Resolving Conflicts

To illustrate this three-step process of resolving conflicts, let's take a look at both a bad and good example of resolving conflicts. Jessie and Reaney are participating in their school play. Jessie has been in many plays before, and is really dedicated to theatre. In fact, she plans on studying drama in college and becoming an actor someday. Reaney, on the other hand, is in her first play. She only wanted to be part of the play because her friend Emily was in it. Reaney and Emily spend a lot of the rehearsal time giggling and whispering to each other. As the night of the big play nears, Jessie's getting more and more frustrated with Reaney. It's getting harder for her to concentrate with Reaney and Emily messing around so much. Following are two different ways that Jessie confronts Reaney.

The Bad Example

As Jessie is rehearsing her lines with her classmate, Reaney and Emily begin giggling out loud. Jessie has had it! All of her pent up frustration must be relieved. She stops in the middle of saying her lines and yells at Reaney:

Jessie: *Reaney, would you just shut up! I'm so sick of you giggling and messing around. You're acting like an idiot! Why did you even join this play in the first place?*

Reaney: *Oh just relax! What's the big deal? Who do you think you are anyway?*

Remember the three steps: Have the "guts" to confront, pick a good time and place to confront, and confront the person tactfully. Well, how did Jessie do? She did confront, but because she avoided confronting Reaney so many times before, Jessie bottled up a lot of frustration. That's why she exploded. Next, was this a good time and place to confront? No. Confronting Reaney in the middle of a rehearsal and in front of all their peers embarrassed Reaney and put her on the defensive. Finally, was Jessie tactful in how she confronted Reaney? Once again, no! Calling Reaney an idiot and telling her to shut up was not very tactful.

The Good Example

Jessie leaves several rehearsals feeling frustrated. She realizes something has to be said for the good of the play. She thinks about when and how to approach Reaney and decides to confront her after the next rehearsal. Once the rehearsal is over, Jessie approaches Reaney and asks if she could talk to her for a minute:

Jessie: *Reaney, I've been wanting to talk to you about something. I know these rehearsals get pretty long and boring at times, but I'm starting to worry about whether we'll be ready by opening night. I've been in other plays where we didn't prepare like we should have, and the play was a flop. I know that you and Emily are just trying to have a little fun, but frankly it gets a little tough to concentrate at times. I hope you don't mind me telling you this – I just want us to perform well.*

Reaney: *Gee, I'm sorry Jessie; I didn't realize we were bothering everybody. Emily and I will tone it down a bit.*

Jessie: *Thanks Reaney – I really appreciate it.*

Well, I think you can see that Jessie did a much better job of confronting the situation this time. She had enough courage to confront but chose to do it at a time when she was a bit more cooled down. She also wanted to confront Reaney one-on-one rather than in front of the group. And Jessie was much more tactful this time – she chose her words carefully and tried hard not to put Reaney on the defensive.

Develop Your Leadership Skills

Not every team player can be a team leader all the time. However, taking on a leadership role is one of the best ways of appreciating the essence of teamwork. Furthermore, it is important to show college and company recruiters that you have the ability to lead. In addition, there are many leadership qualities and skills that are great to have in life as well as at work, whether you are in a leadership role or not. Here are some of the key skills and qualities that are developed during leadership experiences:

- Initiative
- Self-confidence
- Organizational skills
- Teamwork
- Conflict resolution
- Time management
- Strategic planning
- Program coordination/event planning

When you take on a leadership role, you develop a long list of skills and qualities that colleges and companies are looking for in graduates. That's why it is so important for you to explore opportunities where you can serve as a leader. These opportunities will go a long way in helping you become the best you!

> "In talking about teamwork, Microsoft CEO Steve Ballmer once said, "At the end of every day, I'd like people to go home asking: 'Did I make the people around me more productive? Did I help them get more done? Did I offer insights that will enable them to do their job better?'" Microsoft calls the teamwork idea—making others great. This means problem solving and collaboration at the individual level, and focusing on being good managers and leaders through strong hiring, management, communication, and motivation of teams."
>
> —*Microsoft*

Become a Leader of a Club
There are many clubs and organizations that you can join and eventually lead. We will describe how you can get involved in these organizations later in this chapter. You may have to work your way up the ladder to become a leader, so get involved early.

Become a Class Officer
If you really want to take on a big leadership role, run for a class officer position

at your school. Your school's student government will most likely consist of a President, Vice President, Treasurer and Secretary. If you're committed to improving student life in school and want to substantially develop your leadership skills, run for office.

Become a Group Leader In Class

Look for leadership opportunities in the classroom. In class, when you are assigned to various projects, volunteer to be the leader of that project team. In addition, many schools offer a leadership or management course. See if you can take a leadership course.

Become a Leader within your Part-Time and Summer Jobs

There are some other places to become a leader outside of school. As you work at your part-time and summer jobs, look for leadership opportunities. Talk to your boss about wanting to take on more responsibilities, and see if you can help train new student employees. You can really beef up your part-time experience by taking on a leadership role!

Become a Leader in Your Community

Another place where you can find leadership opportunities is in your local community. Community agencies often need help. Many of these agencies would love to have a student volunteer to head up a certain project. Later in this chapter, we will go into greater depth concerning your involvement in community service.

Get Involved in Extra-Curricular Activities

One of the best ways for you to develop your teamwork skills is to get involved in after-school activities, sports teams, and clubs. Make sure you get your hands on a list of the extra-curricular activities that exist at your school. Joining the band, becoming a member of a play, or participating in sports allows you to experience being part of a team. You will learn the importance of working together and believing in a common goal. You'll gain experience dealing with conflicts and overcoming adversity. You'll see that when your team is successful, it's so much sweeter when you have teammates to share the success.

Regarding clubs, choose a club in which you are genuinely interested and start going to meetings. During the meetings, find out about the various events and programs your club offers, and determine in which ones you would like to get involved. Company and college recruiters say repeatedly that they want to hire graduates who were active in extra-curricular activities and student clubs. It's not enough to just attend the meetings. See if there is a program or event that you can take a lead in coordinating. The experience you get as a member of a larger team (club) is good, but the work you do in smaller committees really gives you a good taste of teamwork.

Any time that you are part of a team, whether it is physical or mental, you are developing your teamwork skills. The key is to dive right in and give it a shot.

Volunteer In Your Community

As emphasized throughout this chapter, a big part of being a team player is being unselfish and sacrificing your own agenda to benefit the larger team. This is really the essence of community service. Your local community is a type of team and certain members of this team or community are not as fortunate in life as you are. Giving of yourself and volunteering your time for the benefit of others in need is being the ultimate team player!

Seek out volunteer and community service opportunities that interest you. It may be helping younger kids in the community, or spending time with the elderly, or working with people with disabilities. Most schools provide many opportunities for you to get involved in community service. Often times the athletic team or extra-curricular group you've joined will coordinate community service projects. Remember, whichever group you join up with, you will be working together with your peers on a common cause. There's really no greater experience than participating in community service! Think about it – you get to develop skills that employers and colleges are looking for and skills that will help you be the best you while helping people in need!

On a Personal Note...

As a freshman in college, I signed up for the *Big-Brother/Big-Sister* program. I was assigned to a young boy in the local community who had no real father figure. As a freshman, I didn't have a car on campus. However, every Sunday that year, while my buddies were watching football, I'd beg someone to drive me over to see my little brother. I spent every Sunday afternoon playing and talking with him. We kept in touch over the years, and he is now a successful member of the military. I look back on that experience, and without a doubt, it is the experience of which I am most proud. There is nothing like giving of yourself and touching the life of another person!

A Final Point: Know Your In-Group Tendencies and Adjust

No matter what team you are a member of, as you work in groups—especially during the many meetings of which you will be a part—be aware of your interpersonal tendencies. Do you tend to talk a lot in groups, or do you hardly say anything? Are you more of a big-picture, bottom-line type of person, or do you like to work out the details? A crucial part of being a team player is to understand

> "Being a team player is the most important aspect of an individual. We have found when we create reasons for members to think in the term of the whole unit as opposed to an individual that all members of the team rise to meet the challenge. Therefore, better results are achieved for the entire group as well as the individual."
>
> —*Jefferson Pilot*

your natural tendencies and adjust accordingly for the benefit of the group. For example, if you are an extrovert and tend to answer many of the questions and dominate a lot of the discussion during meetings or in class, you should intentionally keep yourself from talking at times so that others have a chance to contribute their views. Pick the issues about which you feel strongly, and let other team or class members contribute and offer their perspectives. Similarly, if you tend to be a big-picture person with hundreds of ideas, you may need to force yourself to offer just a few and focus in on the details of carrying out the ideas. To summarize, being a team player means that you will be aware of the entire team and its members, own up to your natural tendencies, and adjust your behavior to benefit the team.

The Whole in One

- Top company recruiters reinforce the importance of teamwork in the 21st-century organization.

- The essential qualities of a team player are working together towards a common goal and sacrificing your own best interests to serve the greater good of the team.

- Strong interpersonal skills are a must for the effective team player.

- Confrontation gets a bad rap. When handled tactfully, it can be a powerful way to move past hurdles and work together more effectively.

- There are many leadership opportunities in school. Through leadership experiences, teamwork skills are enhanced and many great qualities that employers and colleges want can be acquired.

- Extracurricular activities and community service are great ways to build your teamwork skills.

- Natural interpersonal tendencies may need to be adjusted to benefit the committee or team.

BECOME THE BEST YOU …BE A TEAM PLAYER!

Chapter Four

Career & Life Essential # 4
Be a Person of CHARACTER

" One person a long time ago said that what doesn't kill you makes you stronger. This is true now more than ever. It does not take much integrity or character to handle life when everything is going your way. What sets winners apart from everyone else is how they handle defeat. It is in defeat that you find out what people are made of. "

—*Enterprise Rent-A-Car*

What do you think of when you hear the term "character?" Maybe a more important question is *WHO* do you think of when you hear the term "character?" Now realize – we're not talking about those people to whom we sarcastically refer as being "quite a character" – *That Erik is funny, he is quite a character!* No, we're talking about people who consistently *show a lot of character*; by fighting through adversity, being positive, remaining honest, and working hard to become self-sufficient. Below we will discuss these four underlying qualities that help define a person of strong character.

1. Fight Through Adversity

As the great late Green Bay Packer coach Vince Lombardi said, *When the going gets tough, the tough get going!* There is no better judge of character than how you deal with adversity. I'm sure at one point or another you've heard a sports announcer say, "He showed a lot of character after losing the big game." Anybody can be a great person when things are going well for them. But when you stare into the face of adversity – flunking a test, losing a big game, being broken up with by your girlfriend/boyfriend – this is the true test of character. How you come back and perform in these tough times defines your character! When you think about it, you have two choices: fight or flight. If you are a person of character, you will fight through the disappointments and setbacks and show the world how much character you have!

Ya Can't Win 'Em All!

Remember when you were three or four years old, and you always seemed to win all the games you played? Your parents or older brother or sister would intentionally lose so you could win. Well, since that time, it hasn't been that easy, right? I'm sure you've experienced your share of losing just as the rest of us have. Everybody in this world experiences failure from time to time. But why is it that some people are able to "roll with the punches" better than others? You know who I mean – those people who are able to "get right back on that horse" after a major disappointment or setback. Below are two pointers to help you deal with setbacks.

Accept the Nature of the Game

People who deal best with adversity have accepted the fact that losing is a part of life – and that, in losing, there's an opportunity to learn and become better. I'm not suggesting that you go into a new situation or game hoping to lose so you can become better! I believe that being competitive and pushing hard to win is necessary for success in life. What I am suggesting is that you learn to analyze the situations you're in, and accept the nature of those situations. It's about getting a realistic mind set. Let me illustrate the point using a baseball hitter.

Think about baseball hitters. When they get one hit out of three times at bat, it's been a good day, right? Major leaguers go home happy after going 1 out of 3 at the plate. But wait – if you really stop and analyze this, you'll see that they have failed two out of three times at bat! How can they go home happy when they failed two out of three times at bat? They can be happy because they've accepted the nature of the game. A .333 batting average (1 out of 3) is universally accepted in the baseball world as a "good, respectable average."

As you throw yourself out there, trying for the lead in your school's play, running for vice president of your class, studying to get an A, or trying out for a team sport, learn to "accept the nature of the game." Some things are more competitive and more difficult to win than others. This is a very important concept to grasp before you start applying to college or begin looking for your first job. You see, a typical Job Search goes something like this: no no no no no no no no no no no no no no no no no no no no no YES! That one yes is all you need to get a job. However, the hard part for most job seekers is getting through the *no's*! If you stop job searching because of the rejections you experience, you'll never get a job. Thus a key to success in finding a job is having a type of "mind set" that prepares you to accept the nature of the job-search game: you will be rejected many more times than you are accepted. So, remember to keep things in perspective, take the setbacks in stride, and get right back on the horse that threw you!

Always Believe in Yourself

A second pointer in being able to fight through adversity has to do with your level of self-confidence. Those who are able to "roll with the punches" never stop believing in themselves. If you are true to yourself and believe in what you're trying to accomplish in life, you will be able to get through setbacks. Focus more on reaching your big goals and not on the little setbacks along the way. You must have enough confidence in yourself to think things through, form your own opinions and beliefs, and act on those beliefs. When you begin doubting yourself after experiencing failure, it is much harder to get through adversity and ultimately become successful. There is no quick and easy way to build your self-confidence. It really boils down to knowing and accepting who you are, believing in yourself, and thinking positive. Maintaining a positive attitude towards life and yourself is critical to being self-confident and getting through the hard times!

> "The best way to look at life is that it is full of choices. Everyday we choose to wake up, get out of bed, and go on with our day. What you cannot choose is what happens TO you. A speaker once described change as a moving train. You can do three things: stand in front of it and get run over - this is what happens to negative people. You can stand beside the tracks and watch it go by - much like people that say "That doesn't or won't affect me" and they miss their opportunity. Or you can do what I advocate, jump on board and see where it takes you. You must always search for the positive and downplay the negative. Remember, it is your choice. You can smile or frown. Anger takes your energy while happiness gives you energy."
>
> —*Enterprise Rent-A-Car*

2. Be a Big Person & Remain Positive

Another underlying personal quality that goes hand-in-hand with strong character is being a big person and having a positive attitude. Nobody likes to hang around petty people who are always whining and negative. To be a person of character, you should try to look at the glass as being half full rather than half empty. It's easy to fall into the glass-half-empty trap when you have so much on your plate and you're feeling tired. However, when you are able to stay upbeat, you'll be surprised how much positive energy you'll have. Following are three helpful pointers to help you remain more positive.

Rise Above the Little Things

Don't make too big of a deal over the little things—keep them in perspective. We all have a tendency to stress out over many little things going on in our lives. We have to learn to tell ourselves to rise above it and just *let it be*. Do any of the following statements ring a bell?

"I think she's mad at me for some reason. I wonder what I did?"
"Why does he always do that? It's so annoying."
"My parents are being so hard on me lately. They need to relax."

The little things that happen to you can turn into a bigger deal when you don't just let it be. Whether you are a driver or not, you can relate to a very common little thing that has turned into a big deal for many people: Someone pulls out in front of you when driving.

When someone pulls out in front of you when you are driving, you have two options. Option one is doing what many people do—speed up and ride the bumper of the person who cut you off, beep your horn repetitively, and make obscene hand gestures towards that person. Option two is to just let it be. When you choose the first option, think about how it affects you. Usually the other driver gets angry and retaliates in some fashion. This causes you to get even angrier than you originally were when he pulled out in front of you. Aside from the fact that you are now encouraging a fight and risking your life, you have worked yourself into a frenzy.

Is it really worth all this? Because somebody (who you don't even know) pulled out in front of you and made you slow down a little, your blood is boiling, you are yelling obscenities that only you can hear, and you are risking your life and the lives of others around you. And it usually doesn't end when you park your car. What do you do with that anger? You take it with you. So now, you are a bit edgier and angrier for the next few hours, while you re-live this event in your head and tell your friends about it. Little things can really add up and eat away at your positive energy.

On the other hand, if you had chosen the second option and just let it be, think how better off you'd be. It's surprising how good you feel when you let it be. Remember, it's easy to let yourself get angry in these situations. It takes a much more positive, secure person with strong character to just let it be. Don't let the little things affect the attitude you portray to the world!

Don't Stress Over Being Busy

You can probably relate to at least one of the following statements:

> *"How am I ever going to be ready for that test?"*
> *"I can't possibly get all this done by next Friday."*
> *"Today is a nightmare. Right after school, I have to run to practice. Then, right after practice, I have to meet up with my study group. And then, somehow, I have to find time to write my reaction paper that's due tomorrow morning."*

Don't you get tired of people who always seem to be running around and telling everyone how busy they are? Who is *not* busy? To remain positive, you must accept the fact that you are going to be busy! It can undoubtedly be stressful for you when you're multitasking, but there are ways to deal with it. While telling everyone that you're busy may relieve a tiny bit of stress, it doesn't fare well for your sense of character. It's just not worth it. The best thing you can do to alleviate some of the stress associated with being busy is to stay organized. When you spend a few minutes each day prioritizing your tasks and preparing for the day, you'll be able to take things in stride, one thing at a time.

Take Care of Yourself Physically

A big part of being positive starts with how you feel physically. A psychologist once said, "You are a different person when you're not tired." I know, it's not the most profound statement, but it may be one of the most underrated ones. When you're tired, everything seems a bit more dreary and negative, doesn't it? Why are babies so happy and positive right after they nap, yet so cranky right before they nap?

It's also important to exercise and have some alone time. Exercising is a great way to relieve stress and clear your head. Also, try to spend even just a half-hour each day by yourself. Take a walk, hang out and listen to music, or just lie in your bed. As a student (and later as a businessperson), you interact with many people for a good chunk of the day. It's healthy to take a break occasionally and reintroduce recess into your life!

3. Be Honest and Reliable

A third quality of someone with strong character is honesty. Lately, there have been too many sad displays of the lack of honesty and integrity in the workplace. Because of this, company recruiters have recently been rating Honesty/Integrity near the top of their wish lists of candidates, as you can see in Appendix A. It's impossible to *become the best you* when you're not honest and trustworthy. Gaining the trust of your family, friends, teachers, teammates, and co-workers takes a long time, but it can be taken away in a moment. It only takes one dishonest act to lose the trust of others for a very long time, if not forever. Just look at cheating in school. If you see or hear about a student cheating, that label sticks to that student for a very long time. Below are three ways to work on becoming more honest and reliable.

> **"** Most of all you should be honest to yourself. Anyone can put a spin on a subject or fact to prove whatever they want. Being honest is in the intent and the execution of the intent. Have you heard that the road to ruin is paved with good intentions? Always be asking yourself what is the RIGHT thing to do. Ask: "Does this help me without hurting others?" The worst thing you can do is make excuses. Be honest and look for the solution! **"**
>
> *—Enterprise Rent-A-Car*

Own Up To Your Mistakes

One aspect of being honest, and ultimately a person of high character, is to take ownership for your actions and admit when you are wrong. Everyone makes mistakes, but too many people want to pass on the blame to others. You will gain more respect from people when you step forward and admit that you made a mistake. Think about it. Don't you respect people who take full responsibility for their actions much more than you do people who pass the blame and get defensive? People with strong character make mistakes just like everybody else, but when they do, they're big enough to step forward and own up to them – that's the difference!

Follow Through on Your Promises

Company recruiters want to hire graduates who can be relied on to follow through on tasks and to represent their company in a professional and mature way. There is nothing more satisfying for a manager than to delegate a task to a co-worker and not have to worry for one second about that co-worker getting the task done well and on time. Think about some of your friends or teachers who are always forgetting things. Can you remember a time when you let one of your friends borrow something, and then later found yourself nagging them to give that something back? After a while, you begin to lose trust in your friend. When people are not very reliable, you stop going to them when you need something done. So another aspect of being honest is to work on being reliable.

> " It is important for recent graduates to understand that Project Mangers/Employers have goals and objectives that they need to achieve. It is through leading that they are able to get these goals achieved. We need employees who can take a list of goals and objectives and go complete them. Project Managers do not have the time to continuously "police" employees on what they have done recently. The Project Manager needs to know that the employee will complete the tasks presented in a timely fashion. It is also important that employees be motivated to find-out what they don't know by being inquisitive and asking questions. It is important to know that since time is money, employees/graduates need to know when to ask questions versus trying to figure it out for themselves."
>
> *—PricewaterhouseCoopers*

Stop Making So Many Excuses

Do you find yourself telling little white lies or making excuses to your friends and classmates in order to spare their feelings? Many of us hate to disappoint others, so instead of being honest, we make up lame excuses. And that's a third way we can sharpen our honesty – stop making excuses! Have you ever been on the other end of a lame excuse, knowing that the excuse is made up? Take a look below at a conversation between John and Jacque about going to the movies.

John: *Hey Jacque, do you want to go to the movies with us Friday night?*

Jacque: *I'd love to, but my cousin's coming in from Boston.*

John: *Bring your cousin along with you!*

Jacque: *I don't think she's getting in until after dinner.*

John: *That's ok, we're going to the 9:30 show.*

Jacque: *Oh, but, um, my cousin's not old enough – she's only 15.*

John: *That's ok, my Mom's going in with us.*

Jacque: *Well, um, I don't think my cousin's much of a movie buff. I wish I could go, but ...*

John: *Well, ok, maybe next time.*

Every time you tell a little lie or make a bogus excuse, you're being dishonest and taking a risk that you'll get caught in a lie. In this case, Jacque really just wanted to spend time alone with her cousin whom she hadn't seen for a long while. Would it have been so bad just saying that? Wouldn't it have made Jacque look better if she'd been straight with John? An honest person with character is a person who is a straight shooter. How many times have you heard someone say, "Boy that guy doesn't pull any punches. I can always count on him giving me an honest answer. I don't always like what he says, but I sure do respect him for it"? Of course there are times when it's wise to spare others' feelings, but for the most part, be honest with people and avoid making lame excuses!

4. Become Self-Sufficient

People with character have pride in themselves and their work. They work hard and find a way to get things done without relying too much on others. Today, it is more important than ever to be self-sufficient. It is projected that you will most likely change jobs between seven and ten times in a lifetime, while changing entire career fields about three times. When it comes to changing jobs, do you really think your old company will help you get a job with a different company? Of course not. You'll need to be self-sufficient and in control of your own career! Don't look for people to do things for you, like helping you write a paper or changing your car tire. Think about the adage, "Give a man a fish, he'll eat for a day. Teach a man to fish, he'll eat for a lifetime." You want to learn how to do things yourself so you will be able to do them throughout your life and teach others along the way.

> " Self-sufficiency benefits our company because the people we hire are capable of making ideas happen. Our collaborative environment encourages people to show their initiative, share their perspectives and contribute to client successes. Self-sufficient individuals also take ownership over their careers and satisfaction, which benefits both the individuals and also our company."
>
> —*Accenture*

Company recruiters like to hire self-sufficient graduates. However, what does that really mean? How do you become self-sufficient? You don't just wake up one day being self-sufficient. The key to becoming self-sufficient is to identify the underlying qualities that enable you to be self-sufficient. Following are three essential qualities of a self-sufficient person.

Analytical/Critical Thinker

The first quality of a self-sufficient person is the ability to think for yourself and analyze situations. As you are tested and face new challenges in school and in life, you cannot always count on your teachers, counselors, or parents for the answers. It is impossible to become self-sufficient if you do not begin to challenge yourself and use your mind to think critically about issues. You must have enough self-confidence to analyze issues and problems and work things out on your own.

If you want to develop your analytical skills, make sure to take your share of math classes. Most schools require that you take a certain number of courses in math, but most students do little more than the minimum. Many students believe that math is a waste of time. People always ask, "Why do we have to do math? We're never going to use this in life." Well, maybe you won't be solving complex mathematical equations on your job, but you will be forced to think critically, analyze problems, and come up with your own solutions.

> "Microsoft is a very dynamic, driven culture, where individuals are given a great deal of autonomy to advance the needs of the business. In such an environment, individuals need to be willing to make smart decisions and take educated risks - our culture is not one where you wait to be directed, our culture is one where you are empowered to take risks and lead in advancing a given idea, product or company program."
>
> *—Microsoft*

My sister, a high school math teacher, uses the following explanation when her students ask, "Why do we have to learn this stuff? We'll never use it in the future":

> *During practice, do football players do push-ups and sit-ups? Sure. But wait, I've gone to a lot of football games, but I've never seen the football players out on the field actually doing push-ups and sit-ups during the game? So why do they waste the time doing push-ups and sit-ups in practice if they never do push-ups and sit-ups during the game?*

Just like push-ups and sit-ups help make football players stronger—which indirectly makes them better football players during the game—doing math and solving mathematical problems helps to strengthen your mind and make you better equipped to think critically and solve problems that you will encounter throughout your life.

In addition to taking math courses, take the time necessary to reflect critically on situations and issues that you face and to formulate your own thoughts and solutions. You will frequently come across issues and problems in class, during your part-time job, in extra-curricular activities, and with your friends. The more you get involved – in and out of class – the more that you will practice using your analytical skills, and thus the more self-sufficient you will become. Challenge yourself to think critically on your own, formulate solutions, and stand by your position in a firm, yet tactful, way.

Initiative/Self-Starter

A second quality of a self-sufficient person is being a self-starter. In today's workplace, companies are forced to be more productive with fewer people. In the 1980s and 1990s, this work trend was referred to as downsizing or rightsizing.

Companies do not have the time to take new employees by the hand and help them figure out everything. They are looking for graduates who are self-starters. Companies do not want to have to tell their employees to do everything; they want their employees to seek out or initiate work to be done. If there is a better way of doing things, they want their employees to have enough initiative to bring it to their attention.

> **"I've seen that it's the students or new hires who have the drive or show initiative that are the most successful in being hired. Oftentimes it's more than just completing a required project—it's developing a smoother process, fine tuning, and re-engineering so that next time there is a better return on your investment. It's the sharing of Best Practices that helps to keep IBM "Best of Class" for its employees."**
>
> **—IBM**

The best way to learn how to take initiative is to find something you love or in which you believe and take the initiative to make it better. Join that club or organization that excites you and think of new programs or services to offer. Sometimes you do not have to create new programs, but initiate ways to improve existing ones. Get involved in your community and volunteer your time. Community service agencies are always looking for energetic volunteers to come in and initiate new programs for the people that they serve. Get involved in your student government and initiate change and new ideas. Taking on a leadership role in school is a prime way to develop and ultimately demonstrate your initiative. There are countless ways to develop your initiative – just look around you, choose something about which you are passionate, and make a difference.

> **"Many years ago, an Enterprise employee in Florida decided that it would be a good business decision to pick up his customers at their home or office and bring them to the Enterprise branch. He implemented the policy in his branch and began to tell his colleagues about this practice. This idea became more and more popular throughout the company as others saw what a benefit it was to the company's customers, and eventually this practice became implemented company wide. Because of his initiative and his willingness to take a chance, Enterprise is now known as the company that will "Pick You Up."**
>
> **—Enterprise Rent-A-Car**

Resourcefulness

A third key to becoming self-sufficient is being resourceful. Have you ever heard someone say, "She's so resourceful?" Did you ever stop and think what that means?

When someone is resourceful, it means that they have the knowledge, imagination, skills, contacts, and assertiveness necessary to get things done or figure things out efficiently. Look at the following scenario that effectively illustrates resourcefulness.

> "Being self-sufficient is a huge advantage to someone as she starts a new career. It shows the employer that the individual is willing to take his or her own initiative and be resourceful to find answers to questions and not just be dependent on those around them. The quicker someone realizes this, ultimately the more successful she will become."
>
> —*Jefferson Pilot*

Case in Point: Two Resourceful Classmates
Todd and Tracy, two high school classmates, volunteer in their community. They go twice a week to a children's agency that works with disadvantaged youth. It was getting close to winter, and the head of the agency mentioned to Todd and Tracy that she wished that the agency would have the funds to purchase computers

> "Accenture seeks students who possess demonstrated leadership qualities and self-sufficiency, among other attributes. We believe these qualities are important because if graduates demonstrate that they are confident and resourceful, it may be easier for them to integrate, contribute and start to have an impact from the very beginning of their careers."
>
> —*Accenture*

for the kids to use. Todd and Tracy began exploring ways to get computers for the kids. They went to the computer department of their local community college and met with the head of the department. Todd and Tracy asked if the department head knew any technology companies in the area that would be willing to hand down older computers. The department head came up with a list of seven companies. Todd and Tracy called each company and scheduled a meeting with their respective public relations directors. Todd and Tracy knew that public relations divisions focus on maintaining a good, positive image with the public and surrounding community. During the meetings, Todd and Tracy informed the public relations directors of the computer needs of the children, and also said that they were planning on approaching every computer company in the community to donate old computers. In addition, they mentioned that the local newspaper reporters were going to write a big article in the newspaper, highlighting the generosity of these participating companies. After meeting with the seven companies, they were able to get computers from three of the seven companies. The head of the agency was thrilled. She could not believe how resourceful Todd and Tracy were.

Todd and Tracy were indeed resourceful. They used their contacts and resources in their community to obtain a list of companies. They also met with the editor-in-chief of the local newspaper and asked her to write a feature article. Todd and Tracy knew that this would encourage the public relations directors to help, since it would be good publicity for the companies. They were assertive in contacting and scheduling meetings with the directors and in selling them on the importance of participating.

Becoming Resourceful

The way to becoming resourceful is similar to developing initiative. You have to get out there and get involved in school and in your community. The more active you become within organizations, the more people and contacts you'll meet and the more knowledge you will gain on important resources that are out there. Become active in community service and you will be forced to become more resourceful since there is often little money and few resources with which to work.

> **"** A Peace Corps Volunteer has to adapt to being self-sufficient during his/her service. As a Volunteer, he/she is normally in rural areas far away from other Volunteers or other Americans, and thus needs to depend upon themselves to survive and be productive. Even though there are numerous projects that a Volunteer can be assigned to, the Volunteer has to be self-reliant and have her own initiative to be successful. **"**
>
> *—Peace Corps*

Join student chapters of associations and attend conferences. For example, some Rotary clubs (consisting of business leaders in the community) have a student chapter called *Rotaract*. High school and college students can join *Rotaract* and get involved in leadership, professional development, and community service through this organization. The students also get to meet and mingle with their sponsoring Rotary members. Another way to gain contacts and become more resourceful is to participate in any career mentoring program that your school sponsors. Sign up, get matched with a professional mentor in a career field of interest, and start networking.

Spending time as an intern or part-time worker at a professional organization is another great way to become more resourceful and self-sufficient. Seeking out and completing an internship or an apprenticeship will allow you to experience first hand what it is like to work in a professional environment. You know how a lot of teachers and other adults like to say, "Wait until you're in the real world—it's not like school." Well, even though you may get sick of hearing that, the statement does have some truth to it. While you are soaking in the environment and learning first hand from those on the job, you will automatically become more resourceful.

In summary, becoming a person of character takes hard work, pride, perseverance, self-confidence, honesty, and a positive attitude. What will it take for you to be known as "a person with a lot of character?"

The Whole in One

- The true test of one's character is how one deals with adversity. You have to have the right mind set to persevere and you should always believe in yourself.

- A person of character is a person with honesty and integrity. It's important to own up to your mistakes, follow through on your promises, and stop making so many excuses!

- You must be a big person and remain positive. Specifically, you should rise above the petty things, don't stress so much over being busy, and take care of yourself physically.

- Companies and organizations today don't have the time to take you by the hand and teach you everything. You must become self-sufficient. Self-sufficient people are critical thinkers, self-starters, and resourceful. The key to developing one's self-sufficiency is to get out there and get involved.

BECOME THE BEST YOU ...BE A PERSON OF CHARACTER!

Chapter Five

Career & Life Essential # 5
Be a Strong COMMUNICATOR

"Accenture works with clients to solve their business challenges and provide solutions for their continued success. We seek individuals who possess strong written and verbal communication skills because they will be key attributes in gathering information, analyzing and relaying that information, and reaching end solutions for teams internally as well as for our clients."

—*Accenture*

Communication in the Modern World

Important to becoming the best you is being a good communicator, that is being comfortable with your language – whether you are writing, reading, speaking, or listening to it. Before we learn how to communicate more effectively, let's look at all the different means of communication that are utilized in the 21st century workplace and in our world today.

> **"** Communication skills are utilized every day. Whatever the medium—be it face-to-face meetings, written correspondence (formal or informal), conference calls, etc.—employees are engaged in communication. A company's success depends on communication. Employees face an endless exchange of ideas, messages, and information as they deal with one another and with customers day after day. How well they communicate can determine whether a company quickly grows into an industry leader or joins thousands of other businesses mired in mediocrity.**"**
>
> **—*Verizon***

In Person

- One-on-one verbal conversations
- One-on-one sign language
- Small-group facilitation and workshops
- Small-group meetings
- Large-group verbal presentations and speeches
- Large-group presentations and speeches via sign-language
- Large-group social gatherings and happy hours

Telephone

- Traditional one-on-one conversations
- Teleconferencing (more than two people)
- Speaker phones
- Mobile/Cell phones

Writing

- Handwritten letters and memos
- Typed letters and documents
- Email messages (and attachments)
- Internet chatting
- Multimedia presentation writing
- Web-page documents

Video

- Video conferencing (talking and observing)
- Video interviewing (interviewing candidates via videoconferencing)
- Electronic video clips (sent via Internet)

> **"** Employees must be able to communicate effectively in email (or "mail" as we call it) through an innate understanding of the unique communications challenges of this medium. Email requires careful, thoughtful communication for tone, style, etc. If these considerations are not effectively managed, employees run the risk of having their email messages misinterpreted which creates conflict and slows a team progress in achieving its goals. **"**
>
> *—Microsoft*

You have likely identified a means of communication that I forgot to add. However, this list still illustrates the point that we have the ability to communicate in so many different ways, all over the world, instantaneously. The ability to communicate effectively becomes more important as we expand our communication capabilities.

It Is Essential to Learn How to Write Well

Recruiters frequently tell career services specialists the importance they place upon good writing skills when hiring graduates. They have witnessed poor writing skills too often in young employees. It is not only that the business documents were not crafted well, but also that the documents were unclear and contained numerous grammatical errors. There is truly an art to writing, and it does not come naturally to most. However, as with any skill, the more you practice and gain experience in writing, the better you will become.

> **"** Our consultants must be able to clearly and succinctly solicit and describe complex business processes. They must be able to gather information and provide it to their Project Leaders in the forms of reports and memos that clearly define the current situation. Our consultants must be able to put into writing what their findings are of our interviews with our clients' employees. **"**
>
> *—PricewaterhouseCoopers*

The most common first impression you give to college and company recruiters comes from the cover letter that you submit along with your application or resume. A cover letter is a one-page letter that serves to introduce you and your application to a potential employer. It is the first opportunity you get to demonstrate your writing skills to a prospective employer or college admissions officer. To give you a better feel for what we mean by good writing skills, look at the following two sample cover letters written by a college senior.

Cover Letter Sample #1

333 Charles Lane
Littlestown, PA 11111
May 1, 2003

Ms. Anne Mummert
Recruiting Manager
Koontz Consulting
1601 Timothy Lane
Philadelphia, PA 19103

Dear Ms. Mummert:

I am a senior at Bair College and would like a job at Koontz Consulting. I know I have the skills that you're looking for. I am a hard worker and can just about get along with everybody. My experience at Werner & Associates gave me a lot of good skills. I think I have what it takes to be successful.

Your company is just what I'm looking for. I want a well-established company who works good with a wide-range of clients. I also want to work for a company that will allow me to grow and advance fast. I think I can learn good and move up quick. I'm highly motivated too. And I'm well-rounded.

If you need to get in touch, just give me a ring. I'll expect to hear from you soon. Thanks.

Sincerely,

Bo Brent

Cover Letter Sample #2

333 Charles Lane
Littlestown, PA 11111
May 1, 2003

Ms. Anne Mummert
Recruiting Manager
Koontz Consulting
1601 Timothy Lane
Philadelphia, PA 19103

Dear Ms. Mummert:

I am writing to express my interest in pursuing consulting opportunities at Koontz Consulting. After reviewing your Web page and reading your 2002 annual report, I am very excited about the possibility of working as a consultant for Koontz Consulting. The emphasis on developing a world-class team, creating a lasting positive change, and providing excellent client services are particularly attractive. Furthermore, I am committed to using my consulting skills in the dynamic and ever-changing private sector. I believe that my abilities and interests match these values, as demonstrated by my resume.

Through my relevant professional experience and my work in strategic planning, change management, and organization development, I have gained the knowledge, experience, skills, and self-confidence to help empower companies to reach higher levels of productivity and efficiency that lasts. I am confident that my prior experience in facilitating strategic planning sessions, training organizations on computer applications and budgeting, and leading research projects on topics including transport logistics and customer service has provided me with the skills needed to become a successful consultant at Koontz Consulting.

I have enclosed a copy of my resume for you to review. I would greatly appreciate the opportunity to learn more about Koontz Consulting and its various professional opportunities. I will call you next week to see if there may be a convenient time to meet with you. Thank you for your time and consideration.

Sincerely,

Bo Brent

It is readily apparent that the second sample is considerably stronger than the first one is. The first cover letter is written poorly, contains bad grammar, and lacks fluidity which means the points do not flow well from one to the next. Additionally, the job candidate does not give a compelling enough explanation for his stated desire to work for Koontz Consulting. It is excessively vague. Do you see how the second cover letter flows much more smoothly? Bo better explains why he wants to work for Koontz, and he is specific about his past experience. Furthermore, he shows a greater connection between his abilities and the needs of the company.

One Word, Even One Letter, Can Ruin a First Impression

It is critical that you always go back, re-read, and edit your written work. Online spell-check systems will catch words that are spelled incorrectly, but they don't catch words that you were not intending to use. The following is one of the biggest resume bloopers of all time.

What was intended: Responsible for **running** the entire Northeast chain of restaurants.
What was written: Responsible for **ruining** the entire Northeast chain of restaurants.

One letter—an "i" instead of an "n" gave this line on the resume a whole new meaning. Have someone else who has a critical eye read over important documents you send out.

How to Develop Your Writing Skills

As was noted previously, writing is a skill, and as all skills go, the more you practice, the better you become. Following are some ways that you can develop your writing skills while in school.

Take English and Literature Classes

Most schools require that you take at least one course in English or literature per year. In addition to the requirements, seek out additional courses that relate to English and writing.

Pick Writing-Intensive Courses and Challenging English Teachers

Though most students seek to discover which courses are easiest and which teachers are least demanding, you will benefit more if you do the opposite. You can go with the flow, or you can choose to swim upstream. Look at it this way: Either you pay now, or you pay later. If you choose the courses that do not challenge your writing ability now, you will pay later when you are on the job or in college and cannot put together a well-written letter or report.

Think about the tough courses you've previously had in school. Those tough courses made it easier on you when you took the same subject the next year. If you have a tough teacher in pre-calculus, for example, the calculus course you'll have to take will probably seem that much easier. If your Spanish I teacher had high expectations, Spanish II won't be so difficult. Pick the tough teachers and writing-intensive courses now to help you develop the writing skills you will need later in your career and life.

Use Your School or Local Writing Tutors

Some schools have writing tutors available to help you write your papers more effectively. If not, check out a local learning center that offers tutoring help in writing, or ask an older sister, brother, or classmate to take a look at your papers. Just as it is a great idea for a beginning golfer to take lessons from a golf instructor, it is a good idea for young writers to take lessons from a writing tutor. The tutor will offer writing techniques that speed up the learning process. Plus, your grades will likely improve since your papers are of a higher quality.

Read, Read, and Read Some More

Reading books and articles exposes you to various writing styles. In essence, the authors are serving as writing models for you. It is similar to learning how to speak. Children who speak well and intelligently usually have parents who have spoken well and modeled good verbal communication skills. Conversely, parents who have limited vocabularies often raise children who have similar limited vocabularies. The more that you read high-quality books and journal articles, the more modeling you will receive. This is a process that takes place without you, the reader, even realizing it. As you read, you see first hand how to express your thoughts more fluently and articulately, and there will be a carry-over into your writing.

> " Communication – both written and verbal allows understanding and being understood. It's not only important to have great people skills and relationship skills but equally important to be able to communicate with individuals who prefer to see it on paper as opposed to hearing it."
>
> —*Jefferson Pilot*

It is Essential to Sharpen Your Verbal Communication Skills

Writing well does not come easily, but at least in writing, if you make a mistake or cannot think of the right words to use, you can take time and edit your first draft. However, when it comes to expressing yourself verbally, you usually don't get a second draft. Just as the cover letter is the first time you'll demonstrate your writing skills to company recruiters, the interview is the first time you'll demonstrate your verbal communication skills. Try to envision yourself on your first interview—even if it is a long time away. Following are the exact words from part of a videotaped mock (practice) interview of a college senior:

> **Interviewer***: What are your greatest strengths?*
>
> **Senior***: Well, like, I'm a good communicator, and, um, I am, like, pretty dependable. Um, like, I feel that, um, oh, um, I can get along with, like, anybody. Um, um, I, um, also think, um, um, I, well, I know I can get the job done good.*

As you can tell, it is not easy for most students to express their thoughts while sounding somewhat professional. When you are talking to your friends, you have the luxury of not worrying about how you talk to them. However, speaking casually with friends can cause you to develop bad speaking habits. It is easy to get a little sloppy and lazy with how you express yourself on a day-to-day basis, since most of the time you are not being judged on how you talk. In your life, though, there will be many times when you have to pick it up a notch – when you want to make a good impression by saying the right thing in the right way. Following are some of the ways for you to practice speaking and work on your verbal communication skills.

> "Our employees spend a great deal of their time working with customers, interacting and working closely with their colleagues, marketing their business and representing Enterprise in their community. Therefore, it is vital that our employees have strong communication skills."
>
> *—Enterprise*

Take Speech Communication Courses

Many high schools offer some kind of speech communication course. It may be disguised in some fancy new catch phrase, so you may need to ask your guidance counselor. If a course is not offered, see if you could take a similar course at your area community college. This type of course teaches you the primary techniques that are used to enhance your verbal communication skills. The course also gives you opportunities to practice speaking to your peers and to receive critical feedback from your teacher. Take the course—it is a no-brainer.

Seek Out In-Class Opportunities

Within your classes, there are frequently opportunities to speak to the class on various topics. Sometimes class presentations are structured into your class. Take these assignments seriously and use them as an opportunity to improve your verbal skills. However, there are other less formal times when the teacher simply asks for volunteers to answer questions or talk about various topics or assignments. Jump right in and volunteer.

Become a Leader

Another great reason to pursue leadership opportunities (besides developing your leadership skills) is to work on your speaking skills. As a leader of a club or team you will be responsible for leading meetings and speaking on behalf of the team. This is a great way to enhance your verbal communication skills in more of a structured setting. You will also be asked to give speeches to various other groups regarding your club's mission and activities. Most leaders serve this public relations role and give many speeches.

Practice Communicating During Part-Time Jobs

When you are at your part-time or summer job, you typically are among peers, but it is likely that you are also among full-time professional workers. You may have to deal with customers on a daily basis. This is a great opportunity for you to practice communicating more professionally. Take your part-time jobs seriously and put some effort into how you express your thoughts to co-workers and customers. Seek out leadership opportunities by volunteering to train new workers. Verbal communication skills are tested when you are training others.

Participate in Speech Communication Seminars

Keep your eye out for communication workshops or seminars that are offered by area businesses or your local community center. These workshops are designed to teach you the proper ways of communicating and how you can enhance your communication skills. Call your area Chamber of Commerce to see if they offer or are aware of any business communication seminars.

Critique Yourself on Video

There is no finer verbal-communication training than watching yourself speak. If your school doesn't offer this type of thing, borrow your parents' video camera and tape yourself giving a presentation you've done for class or will be doing. Ok, it may seem a little weird, but if you're serious about enhancing your communication skills, this is the way to go! Think about it: What other chance do you have of observing your non-verbal communication skills and listening to your verbal communication? Oh sure, you probably watch yourself on videos messing around at a picnic or during holidays. However, that's a little different. When you watch yourself in action while giving a speech, you are seeing how you communicate in more of a professional setting.

Face Your Fear of Public Speaking

It's important that you work on developing your verbal communication skills while you are still in school, so that when it is time to graduate, you will be in better shape than our senior mock-interviewing friend was. However, many students avoid speaking in front of others due to anxiety and fear. It is very common to get nervous and somewhat anxious about public speaking. Here are some points to remember in dealing with your anxiety:

- Take heart in knowing you are not alone. Many people experience anxiety towards public speaking. In surveys conducted on things people fear, "speaking in front of a group" many times ranks up there in the top few.

- **You** are your toughest critic. Think about how you feel when others are speaking. You are barely listening, and you're not judging them critically. You're probably daydreaming through some of their presentation. It is not that big of a deal to the people sitting in their seats watching you. Therefore, don't make it such a big deal. Keep it in perspective.

- Keep breathing. When you are nervous, you will likely get tight and take short quick breaths. Take deep breaths, let your shoulders ease down off your neck, and relax.

- Practice, practice, practice. The more you practice, the less awkward speaking will feel. And the less awkward you feel, the more natural you will become. You will become somewhat desensitized to this anxiety-provoking experience the more you do it.

The Whole in One

- In today's world, there are many different ways to communicate, making it that much more important that you learn how to communicate effectively.

- Good writing skills are hard to come by and recruiters value them big time. Take advantage of all of the opportunities you have to enhance your writing skills while you are still in school: English and writing courses, writing tutors, and reading, reading, reading.

- Verbal communication is critical in the workplace. Face your public speaking fears and get out there and practice.

- Take speech communication courses, master your in-class presentations, practice speaking as a leader, and enhance your verbal skills during part-time jobs.

- Make sure to videotape yourself while speaking. It is the best available method of communication training.

BECOME THE BEST YOU ...BE A STRONG COMMUNICATOR!

Chapter Six

Career & Life Essential # 6
Be a COMPUTER WIZ

"Technology is omnipresent in today's corporate culture. Even though an employee may not work in research and development or work in a technology-specific area, we all are customers and users of technology. We use technology to communicate with our customers and with each other. Graduates should develop a computer technology-literate portfolio as they pursue post-graduation plans. They should have a strong, working skill set so that they can provide suggestions for process improvement and efficiency in the workplace."

—*Verizon*

You might ask, "Why do I have to worry about developing computer skills? I think I can be a pretty good me without them. I'm not planning on specializing in computer science and becoming a computer programmer."

Anyone who wants to find a job in the 21st century workplace needs to have a certain level of technical capability—no matter what career field they are in. To succeed in the modern workplace, organizations must be able to access and present information as quickly or more quickly than their competitors do. For example, when an important client needs a report by eight o'clock the next morning, you must have the technical ability to research the information on the Internet, calculate figures, design graphs, and produce a multimedia presentation within hours. Computer skills are also very important to have outside of work as well. Finding the best vacation sites, the best books to buy, or the cheapest airline ticket can often be accomplished much more efficiently on the Internet. We live in an age where access to information is a mouse click away!

The Types of Computer Skills Recruiters Seek from Graduates

It is important to know what specific types of computer skills that company recruiters are looking for in graduates. It's not enough to say, "I need to develop my computer skills before I graduate." To be the best you, you need to identify and ultimately develop the most valued types of computer skills in work and life.

Below are two different sources that will help us see what companies are looking for when it comes to computer skills. The first source comes from the Toronto Labor Market which keeps track of the technical skills that companies have asked for or required in their job advertisements. These were real job announcements posted over a three-year period. The second source is a survey completed by 150 company recruiters at Cornell University, asking them to identify the computer skills they seek most in graduates. Check out both of these sources to get a feel for the technical skills in demand.

According to the Toronto Labor Market, the following are the technical skills for which employers advertised over the past several years.

Number of Postings	Technical Skills
4109	Word Processing Software
3503	Spreadsheet Software
2379	Database Software
1602	Programming Languages
1026	Network Administration
1034	Accounting Software
778	Internet Software
627	Relational Database Management System (RDBMS)
519	Presentation Software

425	Drafting Software
384	Multimedia Software
335	Mainframe Software
177	Hardware/Software Installations and Configurations
100	Payroll Software
71	Call Center Software
29	Travel Software
10	FAX Software

Source: Human Resources Development - Canada

This Cornell University study drives the point further that technical skills are a necessity for those entering the 21st century workplace.

Computer Skills Required by Employers

1. Word Processing	96%
2. Network (email)	93%
3. Spreadsheet (calculations)	86%
4. Database (basic skills)	83%
5. Graphics/Presentations	75%
6. Programming (personal use)	64%
7. Internet (online searches)	63%

Source: Philip Davis, Cornell University, 1997, T.H.E. Journal. This article is reprinted with permission from T.H.E. Journal, Vol. 25, #12.

The Essential Computer Skills

No matter what your career goals are, you must acquire some essential computer skills. Based on the findings of the two sources previously presented in this chapter, the following are five core computer skills you need to develop before graduation.

> **"We are a professional services organization that provides business solutions to our clients. We start with the creation of a strategy and take that strategy to change their business oftentimes through the implementation of computer solutions. No matter what a person's role is, the understanding of what technology can do is critical to understanding what services we provide to our clients."**
>
> *—PricewaterhouseCoopers*

Word Processing

The days when you would sit back in your chair with your feet up on your desk, dictating to your secretary what you want him or her to type up for you are long gone. The great majority of workers today have a personal computer sitting on their desks or a laptop provided by the company that they take on the road with them. Instead of having your own personal secretary, it is more likely that you'll share a staff assistant. This staff assistant will help you and other colleagues in your division deal with large projects like producing hundreds of copies of a report or helping to coordinate a major function. However, you will likely have to produce the day-to-day reports, memos, and other documents by yourself.

> **" In many areas of IBM it is important for our employees to have strong computer skills but that is not the case in all situations. In fact, many programs may be learned after coming on-board through either classroom or online/webcasting formats. However, most new employees have a familiarity with computer programs, such as word processing, that make it easier for them to be trained on more advanced applications."**
> *—IBM*

You need to be able to type efficiently (hopefully you weren't messing around during your typing class in middle or high school), and insert charts, graphs, tables, and other images into your word-processing documents. Knowing how to format documents is also very important. Setting appropriate tabs and margins, using the right type and size of font, and highlighting appropriately are a few of the essential formatting techniques. Look at the sample document on the next page. Check out the inserted bar graph and the formatting. The sales manager realized the importance of incorporating a bar graph in her memo to clarify her point. In order to produce strong documents, you, too, should learn how to insert various images and take full advantage of the numerous formatting tools available in today's software.

You also must learn how to electronically file your various documents in an organized way for future use. For example, after putting a summary report together for a certain client, customer, or colleague, you will want to avoid having to re-create the same type of report for someone else in the future. You'll want to save the documents that you'll use (at least some of the material) over again in some orderly way that allows you to find them and retrieve them later on. There is nothing that impresses a boss or client more than being able to get them a quality document in a timely fashion.

Spreadsheets

The second core computer skill is using spreadsheets. Spreadsheets are used primarily to enter and maintain data and numbers, and ultimately for producing numerical reports. One of the most common purposes for spreadsheets is budgeting. Let's say, for example, that during your first year on the job, you go to a conference or convention in Atlanta. Your boss asks you to keep a budget of

MEMO

TO: Mr. Peter Logan
FROM: Julie Brent – Sales Manager
RE: Candy Sales Report
DATE: March 23, 2003

Mr. Logan:

Per your request, below are the 2002 sales totals per quarter for each of our three products:

Yearly Report (in thousands)

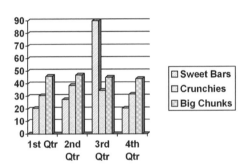

As you can see, Sweet Bars really did well in the third quarter. I attribute its success to our new marketing strategy. Please feel free to call me at work with questions you may have.

your expenses during your 5-day business trip. Following is a sample spreadsheet that helps you keep track of, calculate, and report your expenses:

Atlanta	6/21/02	6/22/02	6/23/02	6/24/02	6/25/02	TOTAL
Travel (air)	250.00				250.00	500.00
Hotel	110.00	110.00	110.00	110.00	110.00	550.00
Meals	75.00	65.00	80.00	90.00	50.00	360.00
Total	435.00	175.00	190.00	200.00	410.00	1,410.00

Outside of work, eventually you'll want to keep a personal budget. You'll have expenses like rent, car payments, food, and entertainment. Using a spreadsheet is a great way to see where your money goes each month!

Another common use of spreadsheets is to keep track of clients or customers. In sales, for example, you may need to keep track of all of your clients and the money that they are spending on the products that your company sells. You could see how you would use a spreadsheet like the one from the Atlanta Conference example to keep track of your client spending amounts. Just know that there will be many instances at work and later in life where you will be glad you learned how to create and maintain spreadsheets!

Databases

Databases are similar to spreadsheets. With both databases and spreadsheets, the purpose is to track information and produce reports on that information. The main difference is that spreadsheets are used primarily to keep track of and calculate numbers, whereas databases are primarily used to store and report on a wider variety of data and information (more words than numbers). You will be expected to design and maintain databases for many different reasons.

Look at the sample database below. Let's say you are the Vice President of your class, and you coordinate the community service projects your school participates in. You need to report on how many hours of community service each student organization has performed. You also need to report on the types of service programs that the organizations have worked with and when they have participated. You see, there are usually multiple types of data that databases keep track of. And from all the different types of data, you can run searches or "queries" to determine specific bits of information to go on reports. Using the community service sample, you can report on—among other things—the total number of students who participated, the total number of service hours performed, and the types of service programs that each student organization worked with.

Service Counter	Date Entered	Term	Service Program	Student Organization	Service Hours	# of Students
1	9/22/03	Summer	Bake Sale	Drama Club	44	15
2	6/10/03	Spring	Crossroads	Girls Soccer	25	10
3	10/12/03	Summer	Big Brother	Football Team	60	20

Databases give you the flexibility to maintain and report on numerous combinations of data types and fields. Designing databases and producing database reports are core skills that will come in handy now and in the future!

Multimedia Presentations

A fourth core computer skill is the design and production of multimedia presentations. The most common type of multimedia presentation is an electronic slide show that you can project straight from your computer. You will be asked to present various ideas, programs, projects, or reports at important meetings, workshops, seminars, and conferences. While flip charts and overhead projectors still have some value, multimedia presentations are THE way to go when it comes to making presentations! Look at the two slides below taken from a career development slide show:

Importance of Career

- Who are you? (9 out of 10 say . . .)
- Why do current students attend college?
    - Time Magazine
- How many will "seek career guidance?"
- Whose job is it to get students to think about their career?
    - College does and doesn't prepare students
    - Students must take initiative

Academics Come First

- Back to the basics
    - Video Clip 1
    - Article: Career Opportunity News
- Academic success is a necessary given
    - Summa Cum Laude, Magna, or . . .
- What are the EXTRAS that make the difference?

Notice the professional look that a multimedia presentation provides. You can incorporate charts, graphs, pictures, audio, and video clips into these electronic slide shows. You can even incorporate hyperlinks from your slide show to an Internet site or some other computer application. Remember the adage, "Image is everything"? It might not be everything, but it is certainly important in our world today!

Internet Research & Web Design

The final core computer skill is the ability to conduct online research efficiently and to design Web pages. Increasingly, companies and organizations worldwide are storing their information and doing business via the Internet. If you want the most up-to-date information on any organization, your best bet is to search the Web. Printed materials get outdated very quickly these days. Companies are looking for young graduates who are savvy users of the Internet. You must be able to conduct online research on products, services, ideas, competitors, programs, people, and much more.

> " It is extremely important for individuals that we hire to possess strong computer skills. Although, most all of our client base work is done face to face, most everyone wants to be able to communicate via the Internet as well. So it is necessary that each of our representatives either have or be willing to adapt and improve their computer skills."
> —*Jefferson Pilot*

With all of the Web editors out there, it is becoming more common for companies to want their new hires to have the ability to design and produce Web pages and Web documents. Large corporations will most likely have Web specialists to design and produce Web pages centrally, but with the majority of job growth coming from small and medium-sized companies, there is a good chance that you will be asked to produce your own Web documents or at least an online form or survey. If you work for a small company, your Web-design skills could set you apart and put you on the fast-track to advancement.

The Internet is also a great tool to use in school. Have you done any online research to help you with a paper or project? You can put together a multimedia presentation and make links to key Internet sites along the way!

Knowing how to use the Internet also comes in handy within your personal life. Obviously, one of the most popular ways to use the Internet for most people is to email friends and family members. It's neat to see how many people now keep in touch with distant friends or extended family members thanks to email. I keep in touch with uncles, aunts and cousins to whom I used to talk only once a year over the holidays! Another time to use the Internet is when you travel. When you are taking a road trip, it's great to be able to receive detailed directions and hotel information by a click or two of the mouse.

> **"**Technology is core and critical to our mission as a company, so examples of utilizing computer skills permeate Microsoft at every level. From Developers and Testers who are creating and testing code on a daily basis, to Program Managers who are making tradeoffs to determine the features incorporated into the next wave of our software, to employees throughout the company who utilize technology daily to execute their work product deliverables, computer skills and a passion for advancing the use of technology are invaluable.**"**
> —*Microsoft*

A word of caution: While email is a great tool, don't go overboard. I know people who used to talk regularly on the phone with certain friends who now only "chat" electronically. You lose a good bit of the "human touch" when you only chat online! I mean, can you really tell how upset a friend may be by his email? The tone of someone's voice can tell you a lot! You know what they say: Too much of anything is not good. In all of life, balance is key.

How to Acquire These Essential Computer Skills

The core computer skills needed to succeed in the 21st century workforce have been unveiled. However, how do you go about acquiring them? Well, as you have seen in prior chapters, you don't have to look far to acquire the 7 Career & Life Essentials. Acquiring the core computer skills is no different. There are many ways for you to acquire computer skills while you are in school.

> **"**Volunteers work with local organizations to provide young people and entrepreneurs with basic training in computer use and Internet technology, opening the doors to e-commerce for micro and small business ventures. By helping people learn more about the power of technology, Peace Corps Volunteers expand the prospects for economic growth in the communities where they serve.**"**
> —*Peace Corps*

Computer Courses

Ask your guidance counselor about various computer courses that are offered to students. You can also look in the academic catalog that describes the courses offered at your local college. There is typically an introductory class in computer science or information systems. If you are not interested in majoring or minoring in computer science later on in college, you will probably want to stay away from more technical computer programming courses. An introductory course in information systems usually will cover topics such as word processing, database design, spreadsheets, and multimedia presentations.

> "Entry-level hires must possess some computer proficiency, e.g., at least one semester of systems or programming. However, given Accenture's strong commitment to training, all entry-level hires will participate in computer training before they are actually assigned to a project. If they are familiar with the programs, it will be all the easier for them in their training courses and also on the job."
>
> —*Accenture*

Minor in Information Systems/Computer Science in College

For you juniors and seniors planning to go to college, you may want to give some thought to pursuing a minor in computer science. If you like computers, but not enough to major in it, getting a minor may be the way to go. Adding a technology minor to whatever you decide to major in will add a lot of weight to your degree. Many companies that come on campus to recruit college students today are looking for students with at least a minor in a technical-related area. No matter what your major is, if you add a technology-related minor, you will be that much more marketable. In addition, you will be more effective early on in your career with this level of computer expertise.

Participate in Computer Training Programs

Many schools offer computer-training workshops and programs to their students, teachers, and administrative staff. Get your hands on a schedule of the types of computer applications and systems on which they are providing training. In addition, if your school does not offer computer training, many local community colleges offer computer training courses and seminars.

Temporary and Part-Time Work

If you are like most students, you need to work part-time and in the summers to make a little money for yourself. While working at Burger King or McDonald's is fine, you may want to look into a temporary employment agency. Temporary employment agencies place people in part-time jobs with local companies. Many of these agencies or firms offer basic computer training, which will make you much more productive. Even if they do not, many part-time jobs require you to perform data entry or work with other computer systems. It's a good way to develop your computer skills. In addition, working at a local company will enable you to network with various employees.

Teach Yourself

Students today are quick at picking up new computer applications, mostly because they've used the computer as a form of entertainment. Most of the computer applications and systems today are very user-friendly, and many have online tutorials. You can often pick up a computer application easily just by playing around with it. And as you're learning a new application, put it to use right away. You don't have to make a fake spreadsheet or database when learning how to develop spreadsheets and databases; you can make one that you actually can get some use out of. For example, if you wanted to have all of your friends' addresses and phone numbers in one, easy to access place, all that you would need to do is create a simple database and enter all of your friends' names, addresses, phone numbers, and email addresses. Once you enter them, you will be able to search quickly for contact information as you need it. In addition, when you want to send out party invitations or holiday cards, you can print your friends' names and addresses directly onto mailing labels. Do the same with word processing, multimedia presentations, and with designing Web pages. Make your own Web page with your favorite links and graphics. Play around with the software and teach yourself. You will be surprised how fun it is to learn new software.

> **"We have unique technology in our branches that has been developed specifically for our rental operations, and it is helpful if our employees are able to learn how to use the system quickly and understand the technological processes that we design."**
> *—Enterprise Rent-A-Car*

The Whole in One

- Company recruiters reinforce the importance of all students developing computer skills.

- Five core computer skills are:
  1. Word processing
  2. Databases
  3. Spreadsheets
  4. Multimedia presentations
  5. Internet research and Web design

- There are many ways to develop the core computer skills:
  1. Take Classes
  2. Minor in information systems
  3. Seek out computer training programs
  4. Develop computer skills while working at temporary or part-time jobs
  5. Teach yourself

BECOME THE BEST YOU ...BE A COMPUTER WIZ!

Chapter Seven

Career & Life Essential # 7
Be an ACTIVE EXPLORER

" We are a fast paced organization that looks to people to be able to learn quickly. We have found that those graduates who have explored and worked in professional environments prior to graduation have shorter learning curves than those who don't. As the old saying goes, time is money. The less time it takes for someone to learn the quicker they become productive. In addition, there are primary professional skills and abilities that are only learned by being a part of an organization. Internships and co-ops in particular help an individual learn what it is like to be in a professional environment. "

—PrciewaterhouseCoopers

You Can Only Choose From What You Know!

Robert Frost wrote, "Two roads diverged in a wood, and I ... I took the one less traveled, and that has made all the difference." Unfortunately, when making important life decisions, most teens aren't exposed to "the road less traveled," and are forced to choose to make decisions based only on those options that have become familiar to them. For instance, if you're looking to buy a music CD, chances are you'll buy a CD that a friend told you about or that you heard on the radio. Out of the thousands of CD's that are out there, it's likely that there's one that would be perfect for you, but because you haven't been exposed to it, you don't buy it. Similarly, most students choose a career based on the small number of options to which they have become exposed. People have been choosing careers in this manner for a long time. Look at what Dr. Charles Moore, author of The Career Game, wrote in 1976, and then what Dr. Jack Rayman, Director of Career Services at Penn State University, wrote over 25 years later in 2002:

Moore, 1976

"It became clear that most of the students who already had prospective career fields in mind had unnecessarily narrowed their initial career selections rather arbitrarily and haphazardly. The federal government's Dictionary of Occupational Titles lists 35,000 separate vocational categories. Nevertheless, I found that most students who selected a career had selected it from among a handful of opportunities they had become familiar with largely through chance circumstances. Some had chosen their major simply because of the rapport they had with a particular professor. Or their parents, relatives, or someone else had decided for them. Most of them knew too little about themselves. Their knowledge of specific career opportunities was limited in most cases to a shallow understanding of their parents', relatives', and friends' occupations and miscellaneous facts they had picked up here and there. Virtually none of these students understood how to approach their career decision strategically."

Source: The Career Game. Ansonia Station, NY: National Institute of Career Planning

Rayman, 2002

"Today's students don't realize that there are more than 22,000 different jobs available within the U.S. economy. Most students' knowledge of the world of work is based on superficial mass-media exposure to a relatively small number of unrepresentative jobs. A surprising number of students don't even know what their parents do for a living. Unfortunately, as a society, we still do a relatively poor job of providing our sons and daughters with exposure to the thousands of different exciting career possibilities that exist. In my opinion the chief obstacle to the consideration of a broader, more representative range of career options is the lack of exposure. We are little

removed from a caste structure with respect to occupational choice. It is still the case that far too many students enter the same occupation as their parents, not because it is an appropriate choice, but because they simply don't know what else is available."

Actively Explore Your Options – Your Future Depends on It!

You will be faced with many important decisions in your life that have a big impact on who you become. It's been said that, *you make decisions, and then the decisions make you.* In order to become the best you, it's critical to be active in exploring your options when you have an important decision to make. Take a look at the following scenario – buying a car – and notice the five steps used in actively exploring the options.

A Model for Actively Exploring: Buying a Car

Let's think ahead about an exciting decision that you'll be making some day— deciding on the right car to buy. There are hundreds and hundreds of cars out there from which to choose; expensive, economical, sporty, practical, big, small, convertibles, SUVs, etc. How can you possibly check out each one? Well, you can't. Therefore, you start by thinking of important things you want in a car, thus eliminating hundreds of others out there (STEP 1). You may say, "I want a sporty car with fewer than 30,000 miles on it. And it can't cost more than $25,000." You now narrowed down your choices and began focusing in on a certain category of cars. Now what?

Well, you first want to start reading up on your options (STEP 2). You can pick up brochures from various local car dealerships and browse through them. Lately, more and more people are heading to the Internet to check out cars. Either way, you will start identifying models of cars that fit your criteria, and you'll read whatever blurbs are available in the brochures or Internet sites. You can take it a step further and read up on these models of interest in various automobile consumer reports. You will get the good and the bad of every car in which you are interested. Well, are you done? Is this all you need to do to buy the car of your dreams? Not usually. Most people are not ready to plunk down thousands of dollars on a car solely from reading a brochure!

The next step may be for you to start asking questions about some of these car prospects (STEP 3). You could talk to a friend or family member who knows more about cars than you do. Alternatively, you can simply call a car dealership to speak with a salesperson and ask questions about the cars you're interested in. Once you get the opinions of other people and get some of your questions answered, you should be ready to buy a car, right? Not really. At this point, most people are still not prepared to buy a car. What's left to do? You'll probably want to go to one or more of the local car dealerships and get a first-hand look at these vehicles (STEP 4). Therefore, you head over to a car lot, and you go over to the section of the lot where the type of car you are looking for will be. You look

BECOMING THE BEST ME

closely over each car, checking out the color, the shape, the interior, and of course, the price. Usually a car salesperson will spot you and start hanging around. You can get more information from the salesperson.

Remember, this is only the first car dealership you have visited. This process may repeat itself multiple times. Anyway, after all of this—surfing the Internet, reading up on cars, talking to friends, asking questions to car salespeople, and getting a first-hand look yourself at many different cars, you're still not ready to make the final decision. There is still typically one last step—the test drive (STEP 5). Most car buyers are not ready to buy a car until they check it out first hand and take it for a test drive! Look at all that is done in order to actively explore cars and make an educated decision on buying the right one.

No matter what you're deciding – what college to attend, what club to join, what internship to acquire, or what career to choose – make sure that you go through the five steps identified in the car model above in order to actively explore your options and make good decisions!

The five steps of an Active Explorer:

❶ **Identify** important criteria of your options
❷ **Read** about your options
❸ **Talk** to people about your options
❹ **Look** at your options
❺ **Experience** your options directly

Actively Exploring Careers

The five-step model for actively exploring is easy to see in the car example above, and should be applied to all of the important decisions in your life. One of the most important decisions you will be making is that of choosing a career. As was mentioned in chapter four, you will be changing jobs and careers many more times than your parents and grandparents did, so it's extra important that you know how to make informed career decisions! Therefore, our remaining points related to being an active explorer will be applied to deciding on a career. Below is a breakdown of the five-step model as it relates to choosing a career.

Step 1: Identify Important Criteria you want in a Career

The first thing you must do in deciding on a career is to reflect on your past and assess yourself. In the career world, this process is called self-assessment. Remember, there are more than 20,000 occupations out there. To begin narrowing down and focusing in on a more manageable number, you must identify what's important to you in a career and eliminate thousands of options that don't fit.

This self-assessment process can be broken down into four main areas: skills, interests, values, and personal qualities. Simply put, skills are things you're good at (speaking, organizing, drawing, etc.), interests are things you enjoy doing (writing, music, sports, etc.), values are what's important to you (family, money, prestige, etc.), and personal qualities are characteristics that best represent who you are (funny, outgoing, caring, etc.).

Talk to your guidance counselor to see what types of self-assessment instruments and exercises your school offers, and take full advantage of them! It's very important that you're honest with yourself in identifying your skills, interests, values and qualities. Too many students kid themselves into believing that they are something that they are not. Another important point to remember is that you should always have a professional career counselor or guidance counselor help you interpret the results of any self-assessment instrument. These counselors are trained to properly interpret these instruments.

Step 2: Read About Career Options of Interest

Now that you have identified your skills, interests, personal qualities and values, you have eliminated hundreds and hundreds of career options and narrowed your search. The next step to choosing a career that is right for you is to read about those careers that interest you. Too often, the title of a career sounds good, but once you read more about it, you may determine that it's not a good fit.

Books About Exploring Careers

The most traditional way to read about careers is to pick up a book. Several books out there describe a wide variety of careers. Two main types of books exist. First, there are the all-inclusive, comprehensive books that will present hundreds of career options. Two of the most highly used books of this kind have historically been, *The Occupational Outlook Handbook* and *The Dictionary of Occupational Titles*, both produced by the U.S. Department of Labor.

If you don't really have a single career field of interest, these comprehensive books are a good start. However, if you have a career in mind, you may want to read the second type of book—the field-specific career exploration books. Many books out there describe occupations within one particular career field. They will be titled something similar to *Careers in Biology* or *Sociology Jobs*.

Most of the career exploration books provide a general overview of the career, education and training required, job availability outlook, salary and earnings, and other useful information. Check with your career education coordinator or guidance counselor to see what types of career exploration books they have.

Internet Sites for Researching Careers

As you may have guessed, there are now Internet sites that enable you to read up on and explore careers. The nice thing about the Internet is that it can spice up this process of exploring careers since it's not just one-dimensional. These sites often add graphics, pictures, and video clips. Two examples of good Internet sites are *www.jobweb.com*, and *www.bls.gov*. The U.S. Department of Labor (DOL) and its Bureau of Labor Statistics (BLS) provides future projections regarding careers that will be in demand. Again, check with your school to see what Internet sites they recommend. Also, check out the Career Center's Web page of your area college or community college. Most career center web pages include a section related to exploring careers that's open to the public as well. Follow these links to learn about careers in which you are interested. The other thing you can do is simply run a search on a search engine like *www.yahoo.com*. Simply type in something similar to "exploring careers" or, if you have a specific career field in mind, like human services, just type in "careers in human services."

Step 3: Talk to People in Careers of Interest

The third step in actively exploring career options is to talk to professionals in careers of interest. We call this informational interviewing, since you will be interviewing professionals for information. Information interviews can be conducted either in-person or over the phone. Some information interviews are even conducted via email these days. Talk to your guidance counselors to see if they know of people in the community that you can information interview. Also, ask your parents if they know of anybody in the careers you're most interested in.

Conducting the Information Interview

There is some strategy associated with conducting information interviews. The worst thing you could do is jump right into asking the person you're interviewing about internships or jobs he or she may have for you. One of the main goals of information interviewing is to build strong relationships with contacts in your career field of interest. The best way to ensure building strong relationships is to follow the **POWER** Model of information interviewing. Establish a solid list of questions using the progression that follows on the next page.

P: Person you are interviewing

O: Organization of your contact

W: Work field of contact

E: Exploration of opportunities with their company or within the field

R: Referrals to other contacts and organizations

You should start your line of questioning around the **P**erson you are interviewing. Ask how your contact got to where he or she is today, and what he or she likes and dislikes about the job. Next, ask questions about the **O**rganization for which your contact works. Ask about the structure of the organization and who their competitors are. Then move to questions related to the **W**ork Field in general. Ask questions about current trends and challenges in the career field. Now that you have built a stronger rapport by asking about them, it is now appropriate to **E**xplore opportunities for yourself. Ask about internships or entry-level jobs for which you may be suited and ask advice on how to pursue these opportunities. Finally, you should never leave an information interview without asking for **R**eferrals to colleagues and other organizations in the field. Ask if there is anyone else he or she would recommend you talking with.

Step 4: Take a Look at Your Career Options: Work Shadowing

The fourth step in the exploration process is to get a closer LOOK at your career options of interest. We call this *work shadowing*. Work shadowing is when you tag along with or shadow professionals at work. You can shadow them for a few hours, a day, a week, or sometimes longer. While you do not get to experience or perform the work directly, you do get to be at the work site and observe what goes on within that career field and company.

You know the saying, "A picture is worth a thousand words." Well, that is at the essence of work shadowing. Through observation and discussions with professionals, you will get a good feel whether this line of work is for you or not. Make sure you are at your best during the work shadowing experience. Ask questions and meet as many people as you can. At the end, ask about possible internships with their company. If you presented yourself well, they may be willing to set up an internship with you. Finally, be sure to send a thank you letter for allowing you to work shadow them. Make sure to visit your career education center or guidance counselor to see if your school has a work-shadowing program.

Step 5: Experience Careers directly – Internships/Co-ops & Apprenticeships

There's no better way to explore careers than to experience them directly for a period of time. Essentially you are "test driving" a career to see if you like it. Many schools provide internship or apprenticeship opportunities to their students, so go and look into it!

> " It is important for our company to hire graduates who have had internships or co-op experiences because that allows those individuals to gain knowledge of the kind of work we are involved in as well as real-world experiences. My experience over the last 12 years tells me that most college graduates do not have enough real-world experience. In most cases college graduates have gone from elementary, middle and high school and their home life to college life. Then from college life they are dumped into the market place with little real-world experience. Internships and co-ops are a great way to gain those experiences."
>
> —*Jefferson Pilot*

Why Internships Are So Important

Internships have always been important to companies. They are a good way to evaluate students and hire those with some relevant experience. However, internships appear to be even more important today than they have been in the past. When I was the Director of the Elon University career center, I went along with the Dean of the Business School to build relationships with companies in the Washington, DC and Baltimore, Maryland area. After visiting approximately twenty company recruiters, we learned just how important internships and co-ops have become. Nearly 90 percent of the recruiters said that because graduates are changing jobs more frequently and leaving their first job sooner than before, they want to do a better job of screening entry-level candidates. Thus, they are trying to position themselves and their internship program in such a way that they will only hire entry-level candidates from their pool of previous interns.

> "The internship program is a key recruitment strategy for Verizon to hire the best talent. Working with interns is a long-term investment for the company in realizing permanent employees. Interns are recruited in a manner similar to how full-time employees are recruited. Through the internship program, the company is able to observe the students -- look at the skills they've developed, see what they've learned and assess what they might contribute to the company's future and its goals. The greatest return on investment is when an intern becomes a permanent employee."
>
> —*Accenture*

This idea makes sense. If it were your job to recruit top-quality graduates with all of the essential skills (interpersonal, teamwork, communication, etc.), it is likely that you would prefer to select a candidate from the pool of interns with whom you worked and whom you observed for months rather than an interview candidate that you got to know for less than one day. It is impossible to assess the work ethic, reliability, perseverance, and appreciation for diversity that a candidate possesses from a three-hour interview. When you serve as a company intern for three or four months, the company gets to see how well you get along with co-workers, whether or not you came to work on time, how you handled conflicts with others, and whether you followed through on tasks.

> "In many cases the hiring manager may assign a new hire to a project based on their previous experience as an intern or co-op. It's one indicator for many of us to really assess a student's interest or passion in a particular area."
> —IBM

Look at the following excerpts taken from various experiential education reports (1999 - 2001) conducted by the National Association of Colleges and Employers (NACE). These reports strongly reinforce the importance and effectiveness of internship programs.

The healthy economy, tight labor market, and high demand for skilled employees have convinced employers of the prudence of sponsoring internship and co-op programs to identify, test, groom, and recruit candidates. The investment is apparently well worth it: More than four-fifths (82.5 percent) of respondents say they offer at least one experiential education program, and more than 98 percent of those use them to recruit for their work forces.

Employers indicated that their experiential hires often became full-time workers in their organizations. Co-op employers reported making full-time employment offers to an average 65 percent of co-ops, with a 67.2 percent acceptance rate. Employers made offers to 56.9 percent of interns, 62.4 percent of which were accepted. An average of 57.5 percent of summer hires were offered jobs, and 62.9 percent accepted them.

Source: JobWeb (www.jobweb.com)— National Association of Colleges and Employers

Make the Most of the internship
Once you are all set and you begin your internship or apprenticeship, it is important that you make the most out of this invaluable experience. Remember, many companies hire previous interns for full-time jobs. This is your time to shine and using the life essentials we've talked about in this book will certainly help you do just that – shine! Show up on time, be nice to all your new co-workers, get your work done ahead of time, and volunteer to do more than what is expected of you. Also, make sure to reflect on your internship experience whether you are required to or not. Maintain a weekly log, expressing what you like, dislike,

and value, as well as the new things that you are learning. In addition, become exposed to the different divisions or departments that exist in the company. Initiate meetings with the directors overseeing the various divisions to learn more about the company. Doing this not only enhances your learning, but it enables you to build more networking contacts for down the road. You never know who may take a liking to you. Get out there and meet as many people as you can.

Reflect on the Experience and Re-evaluate Your Career Goals
Once the internship is over, make sure to reflect on the experience while it is still fresh. Were you able to use the skills and qualities you enjoy using? Was the work that you performed important or valuable? How did you like the work atmosphere? Is this an environment in which you could see yourself working? Schedule an appointment with your guidance counselor. Talk to your career counselor about your experience and how it may have affected your original career goals.

> **"Graduates with internship or co-op experience are able to shorten the learning curve, effectively increasing their speed to productivity. This provides a tremendous benefit to both Microsoft and the student because of a reduced need for initial job training. New hires with internship experience are more effective in hitting the ground running on impactful, challenging projects."**
> **—Microsoft**

Part-Time Jobs as a way to Experience Careers of Interest
Sometimes part-time jobs can feel very much like an internship. However, the main difference lies in the quality or substance of what you are doing. In theory, internships and apprenticeships are intended to be training experiences where

> **"When evaluating an applicant, the Peace Corps considers the "whole person" including your life experiences, community involvement, volunteer work, motivations, and even your hobbies. In most cases, applicants with a bachelor's degree in any discipline, strong motivation and a commitment to Peace Corps service will be competitive to become Peace Corps Volunteers. However, relevant internship will help to set the applicant apart from the crowd."**
> **—Peace Corps**

you're sampling real work you would later do in your career. Most students, on the other hand, do part-time jobs to make a little money for themselves—not necessarily to prepare for their careers. However, if you choose your part-time and summer jobs wisely, they can be a good way to get connected to the real world and sample careers. What you are doing may not be too exciting, but there is nothing wrong with doing a little grunt work or being a gofer occasionally. Also, if you are doing that grunt work for a company in a career field of interest, there is great potential to turn that gofer job into a career-enhancing opportunity. In between the grunting and gofering, sit down and chat with the employees. Ask to meet with various professionals and information interview them. Also, see if there is a more substantial project that needs done and volunteer to assist with that project. Take initiative and make the most of your part-time jobs.

> "We hire many applicants who have held internships in areas such as the insurance industry, and find that these applicants have already learned basic sales skills and have been exposed to a professional office environment. These employees are often able to make an easy transition from a school environment to a professional workplace."
>
> —*Enterprise Rent-A-Car*

Take a Chance and Get Involved

The key to becoming an Active Explorer in life is simply having enough confidence in yourself to get out there and get involved. Anytime you initiate involvement in something, you take a risk of failing. However, if you never throw yourself out there, nothing good can happen. Following is a famous quote from Theodore Roosevelt that helps drive this message home. Get out there and actively explore life!

"It is not the critic who counts; nor the man who points out how the strong stumbled, or where the doer of the deed could have done better. The credit belongs to the man who is actually in the arena; whose face is marred by dust and sweat and blood; who strives valiantly; who errs and comes short again and again; who knows the great enthusiasms, the great devotions, and spends himself in a worthy cause; who at the best knows in the end the triumph of high achievements and who at the worst, if he fails, at least fails while daring greatly; so that his place shall never be with those cold and timid souls who know neither victory nor defeat."
—*Theodore Roosevelt*

The Whole in One

- People make choices based on a limited number of options that they've become exposed to.

- To become an Active Explorer of Life, you must follow the five-step model:
  1. Identify important criteria of your options
  2. Read about your options
  3. Talk to people about your options
  4. Look at your options
  5. Experience your options directly

- Don't flip a coin to choose your career; go through the same five-step model above when choosing a career.

- Internships and Apprenticeships are the best way to "test drive" careers of interest.

- Take a risk and get out there and actively explore all that life has to offer!

BECOME THE BEST YOU ...BE AN ACTIVE EXPLORER!

Some Final Thoughts...

I hope you enjoyed reading about the 7 Career & Life Essentials! Most importantly, I hope you took them to heart and already have begun thinking of ways to incorporate them into your life! Life is way too short to go through the motions and only be a mediocre you. There's nothing worse than looking back over your academic career, your athletic career, your music career, or – most importantly – your life, wondering how good you could have been if you would have given your best. There's no doubt in my mind that if you believe in the 7 Career & Life Essentials and work towards making them a part of you, you **will** *become the best you*!

Remember that the goal is to become the best YOU – not the best HIM or HER or somebody else. Don't try to be something or somebody that you're not! The *best you* may look very different from that of your friend, brother, sister, or parents. While the 7 Career & Life Essentials are important for everybody to develop, you will put your own mark on them.

On that note, I'd like to leave you with a message that was given to me in middle school by one of my role models – a message that has since found its way up on the walls in every one of my bedrooms and offices.

The Man In The Glass

When you get what you want in your struggle for self
And the world makes you king for a day,
Just walk to the mirror and take a look at yourself
And see what the man in the glass has to say.
It isn't your mother, your sweetheart or wife
Whose judgment you must pass,
The fellow whose opinion counts most in your life
Is that man...there...in the glass.
He's the fellow to please, forget all the rest
For he's with you right to the end,
And you'll have passed your most dangerous, most difficult test
If...the man in the glass is your friend.
Sure, you can fool the world as you pass along through the years,
You may even get pats on your back as you pass,
But your only reward will be heartaches and tears,
If you fool...that man in the glass.

—Author Unknown

Be true to yourself, give life your best shot, and I know you'll be able to look in the mirror and say, "I have become the best me!"

Appendix A

Top New-Hire Skills and Personal Qualities

Hundreds of recruiters were asked to rate among a long list of skills they seek in graduates. Following are the top five to seven skills over the past four years.

(5 point scale: 5 = extremely important; 1 = not important)

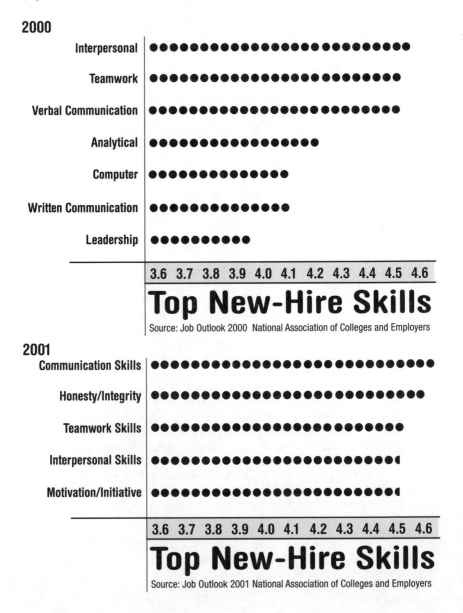

2000

Top New-Hire Skills

Source: Job Outlook 2000 National Association of Colleges and Employers

2001

Top New-Hire Skills

Source: Job Outlook 2001 National Association of Colleges and Employers

NOTE: The Career & Life Essentials that were generated from this first area of research: People Person; Team Player; Strong Communicator; and Character (Honesty/Integrity & Work Ethic)

2002

Communication Skills	●●●●●●●●●●●●●●●●●●●●●●●●●●●●●●●●
Honesty/Integrity	●●●●●●●●●●●●●●●●●●●●●●●●●●●●●●
Teamwork Skills	●●●●●●●●●●●●●●●●●●●●●●●●●●●●(
Interpersonal Skills	●●●●●●●●●●●●●●●●●●●●●●●●●●
Strong Work Ethic	●●●●●●●●●●●●●●●●●●●●●●●●●(

3.6 3.7 3.8 3.9 4.0 4.1 4.2 4.3 4.4 4.5 4.6

Top New-Hire Skills

Source: Job Outlook 2002 National Association of Colleges and Employers

2003

Communication Skills	●●●●●●●●●●●●●●●●●●●●●●●●●●●●●●
Honesty/Integrity	●●●●●●●●●●●●●●●●●●●●●●●●●●●●●
Teamwork Skills	●●●●●●●●●●●●●●●●●●●●●●●●●●●
Interpersonal Skills	●●●●●●●●●●●●●●●●●●●●●●●●●
Strong Work Ethic	●●●●●●●●●●●●●●●●●●●●●●●●●
Motivation/Initiative	●●●●●●●●●●●●●●●●●●●●●●●●

3.6 3.7 3.8 3.9 4.0 4.1 4.2 4.3 4.4 4.5 4.6

Top New-Hire Skills

Source: Job Outlook 2003 National Association of Colleges and Employers

Appendix B

Top Skills Wanted from Job Advertisements

NOTE: The top three desired skills presented in job ads are computer skills, communication skills, and teamwork. If you dig deeper under teamwork, you will see interpersonal skills mentioned as well. Also under teamwork is an appreciation or respect for others and their cultures. This is the first time we saw anything related to *appreciating diversity. Bilingualism* relates closely to diversity as well. Being able to speak a different language is becoming increasingly important in our global workforce.

Thus, two **new** Career Essentials emerged: Computer Wiz and Appreciating Diversity. Also, three Career & Life Essentials mentioned in Appendix A are reinforced here in Appendix B: Strong Communicator, Team Player, and People Person.

Number of Postings	Essential Skills
14462	**Computer Use**
1812	Windows
13152	**Communication Skills**
3836	verbal
3272	written
347	reading text
255	use of documents
7439	**Teamwork Skills**
2740	interpersonal skills
1905	seek a team approach as appropriate
1638	lead when appropriate, mobilizing group
427	plan and make decisions with others and support the outcome
171	exercise give and take to achieve group results
165	understand & work within culture of the group
51	respect thoughts and opinions of others
6146	**Thinking Skills**
4123	planning/organizing of own tasks
1624	problem solving
413	decision making
202	finding information
6	use of memory

Number of Postings	Essential Skills
4519	**Personal Management Skills**
2838	positive attitudes and behaviors
1240	responsibility/management skills
572	works well under pressure
2708	**Bilingualism**
1389	French
207	Spanish
187	Italian
112	Cantonese
103	Portuguese
96	Chinese
94	German
81	Mandarin
78	Greek
47	Tagalog
32	Russian
30	Polish
13	Tamil
6	Somali
1246	**Continuous Learning**
468	**Numeracy**

Source: Toronto Labor Market - Human Resources Development.

This data is collected and updated once per month from the Toronto Star, Toronto Sun, and the Globe and Mail. The postings have been accumulated from January 1998 to March 2001.

Appendix C

Major Trends in the 21st Century Workplace

NOTE: The third area of research examined current and future trends in the 21st century workplace. By looking at trends, it was possible to discover other essential qualities and skills. In particular, *Appreciate Diversity* was the main Career & Life Essential that emerged from looking at the major trend of "Diversity in the Workplace" as seen below. In looking at the second report below, self-sufficiency (an underlying quality of the Career & Life Essential "Character") emerged as well.

Diversity in the Workforce

One of the major trends is the increase of diversity in the workforce. Look at the contrast in diversity from 1995 to the projected diversity in the year 2050.

Ethnic/Racial Percentages in Workforce

1995 (Actual) vs. 2050 (Projection)	1995	2050
White	73.6%	52.8%
Black	12.0%	24.6%
Hispanic (may contain members of any race)	10.2%	13.6%
Asian and Pacific Islander	3.3%	8.2%
American Indian	0.7%	0.9%

In addition, the employment rates of women are rising, while those of men are declining somewhat, and an increasing number of persons with disabilities are entering the workforce as well.

Source: U.S. Department of Labor, Office of Assistant Secretary of Policy

Summary of the Values of Emerging Workers

The one value among emerging workers that is worth highlighting is that the "Individual is responsible for his or her career." If you talk with your grandfather, he might tell you that he worked for the same company for over 40 years and because of his loyalty, that company took care of him with promotions. For the most part, those days are over. Now it is necessary to be self-sufficient and be in control of your career development.

Traditional Worker	**Emerging Worker**
Demand long-term job security	Job security not a driver of commitment
Are less satisfied with their jobs	Are more satisfied with their jobs
Changing jobs damaging to careers	Changing jobs often part of growth
Defines loyalty as tenure	Defines loyalty as accomplishment
Work is opportunity for income	Work provides a chance to grow
Employer responsible for career	Individual responsible for career

Source: Spherion Corporation/Harris Interactive, 1999

Appendix D

Experiences Valued Most by Recruiters

NOTE: This fourth area of research centered around EXPERIENCES that recruiters valued most in graduates. The Career & Life Essential that emerged was Active Explorer. Recruiters want to see that students become involved in a variety of experiences. In particular, exploring careers via internships is the most active way to test out careers of interest.

	Mean* Rating	Standard Deviation	Very Important	Above Average Importance	Below Average Importance	Less Important
Work experience that is job related	1.59	0.84	59%	29%	7%	6%
Leadership role in a student organization	1.81	0.7	34%	52%	12%	2%
Work experience that is paid and job-related	1.94	0.9	35%	44%	12%	8%
Member of student academic or prepro-fessional orgainiation	2.11	0.76	17%	56%	22%	4%
Volunteer community service experience	2.34	0.87	13%	45%	31%	9%
Membership in student social organization	2.71	0.97	9%	31%	36%	23%
Work Experience that is not job related	2.77	0.9	6%	33%	36%	24%
Membership in leisure or hobby organization	2.86	0.81	3%	24%	51%	20%

● Key

1 = Very Important
2 = Above Average Importance
3 = Below Average Importance
4 = Less Important

Source: Journal of Career Planning & Employment, Summer 1998 — National Association of Colleges and Employers; Reprinted with permission from NACE and Florida State University authors: Robert Reardon, Janet Lenz, and Byron Folsom

Employers Rate Experience

1 = not important 5 = most important	2001	2002
Relevant work experience	4.00	4.00
Internship work experience	3.85	3.82
Any work experience	3.79	3.69
Co-op experience	3.21	3.32

Source: Job Outlook 2001 and Job Outlook 2002 — National Association of Colleges and Employers

Appendix E

Using e-portfolios
to Reflect on and Market
Your Career & Life Experiences

Through reading about the 7 Career & Life Essentials, you learned about the experiences that make a difference—internships, leadership in extracurricular activities, and community service, to name a few. Undoubtedly, you will acquire the essential skills and qualities through these experiences. However, acquiring skills and being able to identify and articulate those skills are two different things. Many students storm through school and don't take time out to reflect on their experiences and identify the skills and qualities that are being developed.

As you go through school and become active in various groups and activities, it's important to reflect on your experiences so you can identify the skills, qualities, and interests you are developing. Too many high school seniors are unable to identify and clearly articulate the skills and assets that they have developed during their educational career. You may develop a long list of impressive assets during school, but if you are unable to articulate them effectively to college or company recruiters, you may not do very well during interviews.

One of the best new ways to track and market your experiences is to develop an e-portfolio. For years, artists have gathered their best works of art and put them into their portfolios to show to potential employers or customers. The same concept applies to e-portfolios. An e-portfolio is an electronic or Web document that allows you to gather and organize your experiences and accomplishments, reflect on these experiences, and market yourself to colleges and employers.

What To Put in Your e-portfolio

Whether you are in middle school or a high school senior, it is never too early or late to create your own e-portfolio. Here are just some of the items you can gather and present in your e-portfolio:

- As you write those big papers and complete research projects, add them to your e-portfolio.
- After completing a part-time job, internship, or an extracurricular activity, present a reflection paper or report on your e-portfolio. Start by

summarizing the experience: your essential role or responsibilities, a profile of the organization, and various outcomes or accomplishments. Then reflect on the skills and qualities you developed, and what you liked and disliked. If it was an internship or apprenticeship, include a hyperlink to the organization's Web page.

• List the courses you take each year and give a summary of what you learned, what you enjoyed and did not enjoy learning, and any other highlights of the course. Include the name of the teacher and the textbook. You never know whom you may want to use as references later.

• Add links to other Web sites that interest you. For example, if you love to hike, create a hiking section in your e-portfolio.

• When it comes time to developing your resume, add an online version of your resume to your portfolio. The added benefit of a Web resume is that it is multi-dimensional. You can add links from the first page of your resume to second-level pages and so on. For example, you can have the term "intern" (from your internship experience on your resume) be a link to the company's Web site. This enables the recruiter to assess not only what you did during the internship, but also the type of company for which you worked.

Sample e-portfolios

Two of the best Internet sites for presenting an overview and samples of e-portfolios are Kalamazoo College and Florida State University. Kalamazoo College was one of the first colleges to create e-portfolios. Their site has been a pioneer in the field. The Kalamazoo e-portfolio site is http://www.kzoo.edu/pfolio. Check out this site and the sample e-portfolios it offers. Florida State University's Career Center recently developed an attractive Web-portfolio system. Following are four screen shots of the e-portfolio system presented by the Career Center at Florida State University. Notice how this system enables students to create their own e-portfolio and insert their skills and experiences (screen shots 1-3), and to ultimately produce their final product (screen shot 4). Check out this entire sample online and much more information related to e-portfolios at http://www.career.fsu.edu/portfolio/index.html.

Figure 1: Home Page

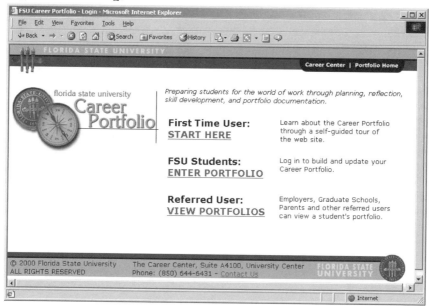

Figure 2: Main Menu

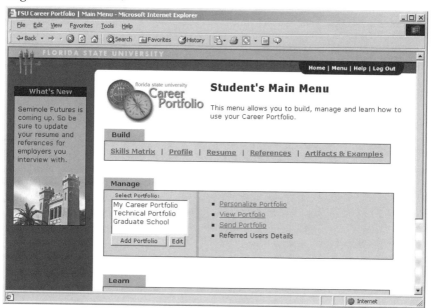

Figure 3: Skills Matrix

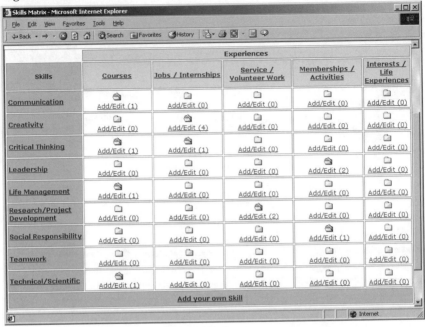

Figure 4: Output of Sample Student's Portfolio

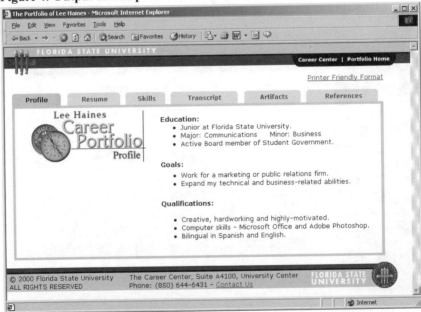

Source: Journal of Career Planning & Employment, Fall 2001 — National Association of Colleges and Employers; Reprinted with permission from NACE and Florida State University authors: Jill A. Lumsden, Jeffrey W. Garis, Robert C. Reardon, Myrna P. Unger, and Scott Arkin

Producing Your Own e-portfolio

Creating the items that you want to include in your e-portfolio is one step of the process; producing your own e-portfolio is another. Talk to your guidance counselor to see if there are any resources in school that could help you produce your portfolio. Also, look into whether or not your school provides you with Web space. Some schools are now providing their students with space on their Web servers to create their own Web pages. If you do not have many resources or assistance, here are five steps you can take to produce your own e-portfolio.

Step One: Develop and Collect Your Portfolio Materials

Identify all the documents, papers, experiments, and links that you want to put in your e-portfolio. Make sure each of your items is of top quality. For example, if you want to include your resume, three term papers, an advertisement you created, a writing sample, and a field study report, you need to make sure each of these items are formatted well, mistake free, and saved on your computer or a disk. Have someone you trust proof your documents.

Step Two: Find a Place on the Internet to Put Your e-portfolio

First, check with your school to see if they provide students with Web space on their servers. If not, ask your parents to contact your Internet Service Provider (ISP) to see if they offer free web space for personal use. If your ISP does not offer free web space, there are some Internet sites that offer free web space. One is http://www.angelfire.lycos.com and another is http://geocities.com.

Step Three: Download Software to Convert Your Portfolio to the Web

Once you have secured a place to put your portfolio, you will need a way to transfer it to the web. Two software packages that are easy to use and are most likely already on your computer are Netscape Page Composer (which comes with Netscape Communicator) and FrontPage Express (which comes with Microsoft Internet Explorer). If you cannot find these software packages on your computer, you can download them. To download Netscape Communicator with Page Composer, visit http://www.netscape.com. To download Internet Explorer with FrontPage Express, visit http://www.microsoft.com/ie.

Step Four: Convert Your Portfolio Materials for Placement on the Web

Most software packages will allow users to paste formatted text. Both of the previously mentioned packages will accept it. Open your e-portfolio from within your word processor and copy the whole thing. Now open the Web publishing software that you downloaded and paste the e-portfolio on a new page. You may want to go back through your portfolio to ensure that the formatting is still in line. The publishing software is a word processor for the Web. Therefore, you can create new documents or edit existing ones within your publishing software.

Step Five: Publish Your Portfolio on the Web

When you are ready to publish the portfolio on the web, you will need to save the file (your e-portfolio) to your computer. If you are using FrontPage Express you will be able to publish using the "Save As" command under the File menu. If you are using Page Composer you need to use the Publish Command under the File menu. You will be prompted to list the name of your file (the name of your e-portfolio) and the location of your file. Fill in the location with the File Transfer Protocol (FTP) location that your ISP or web-hosting company gives you. The FTP location is the publishing location. To view your e-portfolio, you will also need the http or web address. This http location is the web address that you will give to prospective colleges and employers to view your e-portfolio on the Internet. Make sure your service provider gives you both the FTP and http addresses.